THE
ART
OF
REAL ESTATE
APPRAISAL

Dollar$ and ¢ents Answers to Your Questions

William L. Ventolo, Jr.
Martha R. Williams

Dearborn™
Real Estate Education

While a great deal of care has been taken to provide accurate and current information, the ideas, suggestions, general principles and conclusions presented in this text are subject to local, state and federal laws and regulations, court cases and any revisions of same. The reader is thus urged to consult legal counsel regarding any points of law—this publication should not be used as a substitute for competent legal advice.

Publisher: Kathleen A. Welton
Acquisitions Editor: Patrick J. Hogan
Associate Editor: Karen A. Christensen
Senior Project Editor: Jack L. Kiburz
Interior Design: Mary Kushmir
Cover Design: Mary Kushmir

© 1992 by Dearborn Financial Publishing, Inc.

Published by Dearborn Financial Publishing, Inc.

Printed in the United States of America

10   9

Library of Congress Cataloging-in-Publication Data

Ventolo, William L.
    The art of real estate appraisal : dollars and cents answers to
your questions / William L. Ventolo, Jr., Martha R. Williams.
        p.   cm.
    Includes index.
    ISBN 0-79310-207-3 (pbk.)
    1. Real property—Valuation.   I. Williams, Martha R.   II. Title.
    HD1387.V44   1992
    333.33′2—dc20   92-11627
                                                                          CIP

Contents

Preface

Just as financing is essential to almost all real estate transactions, so is the specialized area of appraisal. An appraisal is a supportable estimate or opinion of value. A reliable estimate of the value of property is sought for many different reasons. The seller wants to know the value of his or her property to determine an appropriate selling price; the buyer will rely on an accurate appraisal to be sure the property is fairly priced by the seller; and the broker wants to realize the maximum commission on the sale. In addition, financial institutions insist on an appraisal to determine the amount of money they should lend to a credit applicant. Appraisals also are used to determine value for taxation and insurance purposes, as well as for condemnation proceedings.

The Art of Real Estate Appraisal provides a first exposure to the principles and techniques of appraising residential properties. Assuming that the reader has no prior knowledge of appraising, the book is designed to help homeowners, agents and investors relate appraisal theory and techniques to their practical concerns of home values.

Accurate appraising is a highly developed skill, perhaps even an art in some cases, and we have no illusions that we can turn you into a professional appraiser in a handful of pages. We will, however, tell you a little bit about the theory behind appraising, how professional appraisers go about it and how you, as a prospective real estate professional or homeowner, can perhaps adapt some of their techniques in making your own rough determination of property value.

Introduction

When property values are rising, there are few complaints or concerns about appraisals. When values decline, as has been the case in many parts of the country recently, property appraisals receive considerably more interest.

The collapse of a startling number of savings and loan associations has revealed many abusive practices. The sad fact has been that faulty, and sometimes fraudulent, appraisals were at the heart of many ill-conceived financing schemes. In some cases, apparently, the appraisals were at the request of the lending institution acting in concert with the developer, who often had an ownership interest in the institution. The chicanery was not limited to commercial properties, either. In Florida, entire housing tracts were promoted and sold using highly questionable, if not out-and-out falsified, appraisal data.

Unfortunately, the ultimate victim most often is the property owner. If price appreciation doesn't make up the difference between an inflated appraisal and the true market value, the loss comes out of the homeowner's pocket when the property is sold.

Inflated appraisals combined with low down payments have begun to backfire on lenders, however, as many homeowners with loans for more than their property is worth are simply walking away from their mortgages.

Alarmed, the Federal National Mortgage Association (FNMA, Fannie Mae) and the Federal Home Loan Mortgage Corporation (FHLMC, Freddie Mac), as well as the Veterans Administration (VA) and the Federal Housing Administration (FHA), are acting to improve the appraisal process. The attention that is being focused on the problem undoubtedly has caused many lenders to tighten up their standards. New regulations have been developed by the federal government to transform the appraisal field from its previous, virtually unregulated state to one with uniform professional standards, mandatory licensing and stiff penalties for wrongdoing.

As of January 1, 1993, appraisers involved in certain federally related transactions must be licensed or certified by the state in which the property is located.

The Art of Real Estate Appraisal was written in response to the need for a layman's explanation of the basics of the appraisal process. Because almost every aspect of the real estate business involves appraising, this book can be a useful learning tool, not only for prospective appraisers, but for brokers, salespeople, property managers, investors and speculators as well. Knowing the basics of the appraisal process, for example, can help the real estate agent prepare a comparative market analysis (CMA). This is a service performed by the agent for the seller to determine the approximate market value range of the seller's property. A CMA is a simple version of the sales comparison approach, one of three ways to estimate real estate value in a formal appraisal.

Readers interested in buying or selling their own homes, refinancing their mortgage or remodeling for value will find *The Art of Real Estate Appraisal* equally useful. If you are a homeseller, learning as much as you can about the appraisal process can help you set a realistic asking price for your property. If you are a homebuyer, an understanding of the appraisal process will help you determine a fair offering price for the home you want to buy. A good working knowledge of the basic principles of property valuation also may be helpful when judging the accuracy of your tax assessment or considering a home improvement project.

Your effort, however, never should replace the services of a professional appraiser. Too many factors are involved in making an appraisal estimate for you to risk your limited knowledge on what probably is the biggest investment of your life.

In conclusion, you won't find out all there is to know about appraising by reading through this book. However, if we can explain how real estate values are determined and what some of the problems are in arriving at a fair market value, we will have accomplished our purpose.

1

Real Estate and Its Appraisal

An accurate appraisal is the basis for the transfer of property—either the buying or the selling of it. A much more important function of appraisals, however, is to assist lenders in making mortgage loan decisions. That, as a matter of fact, is the area in which most appraisal work being conducted today takes place.

In 1932, the American Institute of Real Estate Appraisers was organized, and in 1935, the Society of Residential Appraisers was organized. Both groups came into being primarily to satisfy the needs of the lender, not those of the buyer or seller.

WHAT IS A REAL ESTATE APPRAISAL?

In theory, at least, appraising is a simple concept to grasp. An appraisal is a supportable estimate of property value. It includes a description of the property under consideration and the appraiser's opinion of the property's condition, its utility for a given purpose and/or its probable monetary value on the open market. Because it is only an estimate, the worth of any appraisal depends on the skill, experience and good judgment of the person making the appraisal. With an objective, well-researched and carefully documented appraisal, all parties involved, whether in a sale, a proposed mortgage loan or other transaction, are aided in the decision-making process.

All real estate appraisals are based on data obtained from the marketplace. The probable value of a piece of real estate may be affected by national and even international conditions. Population changes, government fiscal policies, business and industry trends, inflation, high interest rates and types of loans currently available, all have a direct bearing on the value of real estate.

Economic characteristics and trends of the city or area in which a property is located are other factors to be considered when estimating the value of real estate. Most important in an appraisal is a comprehensive analysis of the neighborhood. Every piece of property is affected by its surroundings and by the uses to which other properties in the neighborhood or market area are put. In the final value estimate, neighborhood analysis is as important as the special characteristics of the property under appraisal.

To produce a reasonably accurate estimate of value, the appraiser must compile all relevant data, assemble it in an orderly manner and use standard procedures and techniques developed through the experience of the appraisal profession. Thus, an appraisal is a combination of fact findings, sound judgment and past experience.

In each real estate transaction, the appraiser should act as a disinterested third party and compensation should not be contingent on the amount of the value estimate. With no financial interest in the property and nothing to gain or lose from the outcome of the appraisal, the appraiser should be able to objectively evaluate the property's relative merits, appeal and value.

LAND VERSUS SITE

Land is commonly thought of as the ground or soil. From a legal standpoint, however, land refers to the earth's surface and everything under or on it and, within limitations, the air rights above it.

A residential **site,** on the other hand, is land plus improvements that make the land ready for the construction of a house, apartment building or other structure. Site improvements may include clearing, grading, landscaping, drainage systems, sewers, utility connections (water, gas, electricity), sidewalks, curbs, streetlights and access to roads. Figure 1.1 can be used to note the features of a site.

REAL ESTATE AND REAL PROPERTY

To begin the study of real estate appraisal, an important distinction must be made between the terms *real estate* and *real property*. **Real estate** refers to the physical, tangible land and all things permanently attached to it, called fixtures. **Real property** refers to the rights of ownership of the physical real estate—often called the bundle of rights. Included in the bundle are the rights to use, sell, rent or give away the real estate as well as to choose *not* to exercise any of these rights.

FIGURE 1.1 Site Features

	Yes	No
Landscaping	_____	_____
Drainage systems	_____	_____
Water	_____	_____
Gas	_____	_____
Electricity	_____	_____
Sidewalks	_____	_____
Curbs	_____	_____
Sewers	_____	_____
Streetlights	_____	_____
Access to roads	_____	_____
_____	_____	_____
_____	_____	_____
_____	_____	_____

An individual doesn't actually own the real estate—the physical thing. It is the bundle of rights inherent in the ownership of real estate that may be bought and sold in a real estate transaction.

Although the concepts are different, the terms *real estate* and *real property* often are used interchangeably. In some states, such as California, the terms are considered synonymous.

PUBLIC RESTRICTIONS

Four basic public limitations are placed on the private ownership of real estate. These are:

1. *Taxation.* The power to tax the real estate for the support of the government and to sell the property if taxes are not paid.
2. *Eminent domain.* The power to take private property for public use, provided just compensation is paid.
3. *Police power.* The right of government to establish building codes, zoning ordinances, traffic regulations and other measures that restrict the use of real estate to protect the health, safety, morals and general welfare of the public.
4. *Escheat.* The power to have property revert to the state if the owner dies leaving no qualified heirs.

OTHER RESTRICTIONS ON LAND USE

Deed restrictions, which the buyer agrees to by his or her purchase of the property, perform the same function as zoning and building codes—to maintain specific standards in a subdivision. These restrictions usually are placed in the deed by the original subdivider, although it is not uncommon for the members of a subdivision to vote on the inclusion of a new provision in the deeds for their properties. Deed restrictions normally relate to: type of building; land use; type of construction, height, setbacks and square footage; and cost.

Easements impose other restrictions on land use. An **easement** is a right of ingress, egress or use of property that an owner grants to others. The owner of a lake lot, for example, may grant an easement so that the owner of an adjacent lot can have lake access. Or an owner may be prohibited from building on any part of the property that provides access to utility installations. Any easements will be included in a property's legal description.

PERSONAL PROPERTY

Appraisers also must differentiate between real estate and personal property. **Personal property** refers to tangible items not permanently attached to or part of the real estate and thus such items are not considered fixtures. To determine whether an item should be considered personal property or real estate, appraisers and the courts generally use the following criteria:

1. How the item is attached (permanent or nonpermanent) and
2. The intent of the person who attached it (to leave the item permanently or to remove it at some future date).

Generally speaking, an item remains personal property if it can be removed without serious injury either to the real estate or to the item itself. For example, a window air conditioner ordinarily would be considered personal property, but if a hole were cut in a wall expressly for the installation of the air conditioner, the unit probably would be considered part of the real estate—a fixture.

Items of personal property usually are not included in a real estate appraisal. The parties involved in a transaction should agree on whether to consider an item to be part of the real estate. The best way to avoid disputes is to list all items that might cause controversy. In the absence of such an agreement, however, legal action ultimately might decide the issue. If litigation is necessary because it is unclear whether an item is a fixture or personal property, the courts generally will favor the buyer over the seller and the lender over the borrower.

Figure 1.2 can be used to list all personal property items and fixtures found in the home. To avoid misunderstandings later on, both the buyer and the seller should initial each item to indicate agreement.

FIGURE 1.2 Personal Property

Personal Property	Fixtures	Agreement
_____	_____	_____
_____	_____	_____
_____	_____	_____
_____	_____	_____
_____	_____	_____
_____	_____	_____
_____	_____	_____
_____	_____	_____
_____	_____	_____
_____	_____	_____

Controversial items to be negotiated:

_____

_____

_____

_____

_____

2

The Real Estate Marketplace

HISTORICAL BACKGROUND

In the United States, the market for real estate in the post–World War II era has benefited from record high levels of demand and subsequent price appreciation for both new and existing homes and commercial properties. What goes up can come down, however, as every economist and most homeowners can verify. The past decade serves as a textbook example of economic forces and their effect on the marketplace.

The Ecstasy and the Agony

Encouraged by the growing needs of the maturing baby boomers and an expanding economy, as well as by tax laws that favored investment, record high levels of building occurred during the 1980s. Unfortunately, the cresting wave of demand for housing and commercial development began its inevitable slide down just as the Tax Reform Act of 1986 removed many of the incentives for real estate investment. In addition, many areas of the country that had been riding high on the fortunes of specialized industries, from oil and gas to high-tech products and services, suffered the effects of overcompetition and reduced market prices. What had been reasonably based expectations when many development projects were started were turned around so completely that the tenantless "see-through" office building became commonplace.

The downturn of the real estate market also was both cause and effect of the major economic scandal of this half-century—the

7

collapse of a large segment of the savings and loan industry. With the benefit of hindsight, the current problems of the savings and loan institutions are not surprising. Thanks to the Depository Institutions Deregulation and Monetary Control Act of 1982, the lending institutions were forced to compete in a newly deregulated marketplace. The benefit of offering interest-bearing checking accounts was to be measured against the burden of offering competitive interest rates at a time of high inflation. New depositors expected double-digit interest rates, while many institutions were locked into older long-term fixed-rate loans that paid only a single-digit rate of return.

Certainly, greed was at the core of some of the savings and loan collapses, but it was not the only factor at work. Many of the problems experienced by the industry stemmed from frantic efforts to compensate for the wild swing in interest rates in an intensely competitive environment by moving to ever riskier investments. The savings and loans were not unique in having to confront this dilemma. A growing number of banks now threaten to join the ranks of insolvent financial institutions.

Market Controls and Remedies

Few homebuyers just entering the real estate marketplace could afford to pay all cash for their properties. The tax advantages of home ownership usually make an all-cash purchase a poor choice in any event. As a result, the **cost of credit** is a major factor affecting the home purchase decision. Home affordability—the amount of the monthly loan payment—will be determined by the down payment required, the loan amount, the length of the loan term and the interest rate charged.

The central bank of the United States is the **Federal Reserve Bank System (the Fed)**. The Fed regulates the flow of money as well as the cost of credit by:

1. Raising or lowering the **cash reserve requirements** of member banks, which decreases or increases the amount of money available for lending;
2. Setting the **discount rate** (interest rate) that member banks pay the Fed for money that they borrow; in turn, this affects the **prime rate** banks charge their highest-rated commercial borrowers and ultimately the rate charged to consumers on home mortgage loans; and
3. Buying and selling government securities, which also affect the amount of money available for lending.

At a time of high interest rates, seller financing for all or part of the purchase price frequently is used to increase home affordability.

One of the ways in which the Fed has sought to avoid a repetition of the savings and loan disaster in the banking industry is by increasing the reserve requirements of member banks. This tactic has resulted in a decrease in funds available for lending, as well as an increase in the number of banks that, on paper, are teetering on the brink of insolvency. New restraints on lenders also were imposed by the Financial Institutions Reform and Recovery Act of 1989 (FIRREA).

FIRREA created the Resolution Trust Corporation (RTC), which is charged with taking over troubled savings and loans and, if necessary, disposing of their assets. The RTC has had difficulty disposing of its growing inventory of properties, especially because the greatest number are in already troubled market areas, such as Texas and Colorado. Various commentators and groups have suggested seller financing, low down payments and open auctions with no reserve or minimum bid requirement as some of the ways by which the RTC can entice buyers. In short, the properties that RTC must sell must be priced as attractively and carry the same financial inducements as any other property available in the marketplace. Only then will they come close to commanding a price anywhere near their market value.

MARKET VALUE

This book already has mentioned "market value" several times, but what exactly is market value?

Market value is the most probable price a buyer is willing to pay a seller for a product on the open market, in an arm's-length transaction. Notice that market value is *not* the highest price possible for the property, but the most likely price the property will command. An arm's-length transaction is one in which:

- Buyer and seller are not related in any way;
- The product has been on the market for a length of time that is reasonable for products of that type;
- Neither buyer nor seller is acting under duress; and
- There are no financing or other concessions beyond what is customary in the marketplace.

A property's market value frequently is referred to as its **fair market value.** The two terms—*market value* and *fair market value*—mean the same thing. The concept of "fairness" has nothing to do with favoring or disfavoring either seller or buyer, or of being "fair" to either seller or buyer in terms of his or her needs or desires. It simply means that the estimated value is based on an arm's-length transaction, without unusual influences.

Is market value the same as asking price? Is it the same as offering price? Is it the same as selling price? The two possible answers to all of these questions are "maybe" and "sometimes." Asking price is what the seller indicates will be an acceptable offer. Offering price is what a buyer actually offers. Selling price is what the seller and buyer finally agree on. All of these may be different from the property's market value, as determined by an appraiser, and none of them may be exactly the same as the estimated market value. It is not difficult to think of some of the reasons why this is true.

Asking Price

A seller is free to set whatever asking price he or she chooses for the home that is for sale. The asking price often will be set higher than the price the seller is willing to accept to allow room for negotiation. Even the price the seller is willing to accept is not necessarily an accurate reflection of the property's market value.

It is usually difficult for a homeseller to be entirely objective about a house that has been the recipient of years of upkeep. The seller may find it hard to believe that all of the dollars expended in "improvements" do not necessarily add an equal amount to property value. To compound the problem, the seller may have no idea of the actual sales prices of properties in the area. The seller's information may be limited to the asking prices advertised in the local newspaper's classified ads. The seller who distrusts real estate agents may miss out on the valuable service that they perform when conducting a competitive market analysis of similar properties in the area that are for sale or have sold recently.

Offering Price

A buyer is free to offer whatever he or she chooses and often will submit an offer lower than the maximum price he or she is willing to pay to allow room for negotiation. Of course, many factors can affect the negotiation. For example, the buyer may offer the seller a quick closing. Even though the seller is not under any duress to sell, the quick closing (and just-as-quick receipt of the sale proceeds) may tempt the seller to accept an offer that is under the seller's ideal price.

Selling Price

By definition, it would seem that selling price should almost always be the same as market value. After all, if the appraiser has performed a thorough and accurate job in making an estimate of a property's market value, shouldn't the selling price match that value? Unfortunately, far too many factors are at work in the average transaction for an appraiser to be able to make an estimate of market value that will be matched exactly by the property's ultimate selling price.

In some negotiations, the sale price is secondary to other considerations, such as the terms of financing and the date of possession. If the seller is willing to offer financing, even if the financing is no lower than the prevailing market rate, the buyer will benefit by not having to pay expensive points and loan fees to a lender. In such a case, the seller may be able to hold out for a slightly higher asking price. If the seller needs a quick closing, as happens frequently when the seller has been transferred out of the area or already has purchased a new home, the buyer will have a stronger negotiation position and the selling price probably will be reduced accordingly.

Of course, competing factors also may be at work. What if the seller, because of a job transfer, is forced to sell in a "buyer's market"—that is, one in which there are significantly more properties available for sale than buyers available to purchase them? Either factor—the forced sale or the buyer's market—could mean a lower selling price than would otherwise be possible. Together, the seller's need to sell and the inhospitality of the marketplace could result in a selling price well below the property's potential in the hands of another seller in another market climate.

VALUE PRINCIPLES

Economists have identified a number of basic value principles at work in any marketplace for a product or service. The same principles apply to a sale of real estate.

Substitution

An appraiser's work relies heavily on the use of the principle of **substitution.** Property value is influenced by the cost to acquire a comparable property—one that has the same design and construction, or functional utility, as the property under consideration.

For example, suppose that a house on Block A is listed for sale at $200,000 and a similar house on Block B is listed for sale at $225,000. The house on Block A is likely to sell first, because it is cheaper. We are assuming, of course, that the properties are, indeed, similar; that is, that they are alike in terms of lot dimensions and landscaping, size of home, amenities, upkeep and other features. The typical suburban subdivision usually provides ample opportunity to compare selling and asking prices of comparable homes because few design or construction differences generally exist among houses.

We will be referring to the principle of substitution throughout this book, particularly in Chapter 6, "The Sales Comparison Approach."

Highest and Best Use

A property achieves its highest value at its most profitable legally and physically permitted use. Determining a property's **highest and best use** should be a part of every appraisal. An appraisal of vacant land can take into account the entire range of legally possible uses for the property. If there is an existing structure, the cost to remove or remodel the building would have to be considered as well. Existing zoning should be taken into account, as well as the possibility of zoning changes.

The appraiser attempts to identify the economic factors that may make different land uses more profitable at different times. Thus, a study of a property's highest and best use involves an analysis of the community and neighborhood, and how they are affected by national, state and regional market trends, as well as the subject property. The same property's highest and best use also may change, even over a short period. The vacant land that was considered ideal for an office park when commercial space was in short supply may be better suited for apartment development a few years down the road if the commercial market has been overbuilt and housing is in short supply.

A house built on property that is zoned for single-family residential building only is the property's highest and best use.

Externalities

According to the principle of **externalities,** factors outside a property can influence property value. If mortgage interest rates are relatively high, for example, property values may be lower than they would be if loans at lower interest rates were available. If federal mortgage insurance programs, such as that of the Federal Housing Administration (FHA), make additional funds available for lending, more buyers will be drawn into the market and property values should go up as a result. On the local level, the attractiveness of a neighborhood in terms of uniform, mature landscaping and good upkeep of homes usually results in a higher resale value for all properties.

Supply and Demand

The single greatest factor affecting negotiations between buyer and seller usually will be the principle of **supply and demand.** The cost of any property will be influenced by the number of other similar properties for sale relative to the number of buyers in the marketplace. If there are few buyers in relation to the number of properties for sale, the seller's bargaining position is effectively reduced. If the situation is reversed, and there are few properties for sale relative to the number of buyers seeking to make a purchase, the seller can hold out for the maximum price.

Balance

A market that is in **balance** will tend to have more properties available for sale than there are buyers. There always are some owners who list their properties for sale merely to "test the market." Such owners will refuse to sell for anything less than the full asking price, which may be set unrealistically high.

These are the sellers who are willing to wait out the market by keeping their homes listed for as long as necessary, or by taking them off the market and relisting them again when, theoretically, market values have risen. There always will be some properties that are overpriced, but the marketplace is the great leveler that ultimately indicates just how much buyers are willing to pay for the privilege of home ownership.

Property **uses** are said to be in balance when there are a sufficient number of complementary property types; that is, the number of residential units is adequate for the number of commercial and industrial units. A community that has too few retail stores for its population, for instance, will be less desirable than the community that can offer a good mix of shopping for most everyday needs. In addition, the community with too few business establishments probably will suffer from decreased sales tax revenue and other exactions that can help support city services.

Competition

The effect of the principle of **competition** is evident when home values lower as competition increases (more properties are available on the market). It also is evident when home values rise as competition decreases (fewer properties are available on the market).

On the other hand, increased competition may serve as a benefit or a detriment to a commercial property owner. Retail stores always are especially sensitive to the combined forces of the demand for their products and the number of other stores available to supply the demand. At first, competition may be viewed with suspicion as potential customers are lost to another establishment. With enough competition, however, the retail area may become a center of trade and attract even more customers than a single store ever could alone. This phenomenon is commonly exhibited in shopping malls, where merchandisers of similar products benefit from their shared location, particularly when care has been taken to provide an overall diversity of products and services.

Change

Every property is influenced by the principle of **change.** All factors affecting property value, whether physical or economic, are subject to change. The change may be tumultuous, as when earthquakes, fires or hurricanes wreak disaster on wide areas, or it may be as gradual as the routine wear and tear of the elements. The marketplace, too, undergoes constant change. Interest rates, levels of employment and income and other factors affecting demand can change with frightening speed. The professional appraiser must keep up with economic trends to be able to predict as accurately as possible their possible effect on the marketplace.

Conformity, Progression and Regression

Generally, homes reach their highest value only when they are in **conformity** with others in the neighborhood. This means that they should be alike in terms of age, method and quality of construction, design and amenities. The value of a home that does not conform to others in the neighborhood may actually benefit, if the home is of lesser quality or upkeep than its neighbors. This is an example of the principle of **progression.** The general good appearance of the neighborhood can reflect favorably on a home that is not in as good condition. Likewise, however, the value of a home that would otherwise create a favorable impression will suffer if the rest of the neighborhood is not in as good condition. This is an example of the principle of **regression.**

Growth, Equilibrium and Decline

Individual properties, as well as neighborhoods, also undergo constant change. The effects of ordinary physical deterioration and market demand dictate that property will pass through three stages:

1. **Growth,** when improvements are being built and demand is rising;
2. **Equilibrium,** when the neighborhood is virtually complete and properties appear to undergo little change; and
3. **Decline,** when individual properties require increasing amounts of upkeep while demand decreases.

High demand for housing and stringent growth controls in many urban areas have resulted in a new, fourth stage that could be termed **revitalization.** Older, neglected neighborhoods that once would have continued to decline have become newly attractive. Many property buyers have decided that the high cost of upkeep of older homes may be worth the convenience of a location close to the downtown business district and cultural center and, in some cases, the larger lots and increased amenities that are available also may be desirable. This process, also described as **gentrification,** is particularly evident in cities with very high property costs, such as San Francisco and Los Angeles.

Anticipation

Usually, one of the reasons real estate is purchased is the expectation that it will increase in value over time. Especially considering the growing cost of real estate relative to personal income, the **anticipation** of the property's future value is an important factor. Certainly, the vast majority of property buyers would like to see some profit earned on their investment through an increase in their equity.

Unfortunately, the dramatic inflation in real estate values in many parts of the country at different periods in the past two decades may have given some current property owners and sellers a distorted view of the potential for appreciation of their properties. New entrants to the housing marketplace have learned to accept the inevitable outcome of increased demand and decreased supply. The "acceptable" percentage of gross income devoted to housing is no longer the 25 percent that homebuyers in the 1950s and 1960s could expect to pay, but a percentage that is closer to one-third of gross income. That figure is even more significant when you consider that the income figure is typically generated by two wage earners.

The principle of anticipation has not been forgotten, of course. Even the newest homeowners typically expect their property to provide them a nice nest egg some day, even if it is accomplished only by their paying down the mortgage.

Contribution

An improvement to real estate can help increase a property's market value. The increase in value, however, will not necessarily be the same as the dollar amount spent on the improvement. An improvement's **contribution** to market value is measured by its affect on the value of the entire property, rather than the intrinsic cost of the improvement.

Some improvements, such as a remodeled basement, usually will not contribute their entire cost to a home's market value. Other improvements, such as a second bathroom, may contribute more than their cost to the home's market value. Even if the improvement is one that is sought after in the community, the homeowner must guard against making an improvement that is far too luxurious, too expensive or too personalized for the average buyer's taste and pocketbook.

Many homeowners come to grief because they fail to understand this basic value principle. They don't realize that certain improvements may increase the comfort and utility of their home *for them,* but those improvements may not be considered necessary or even desirable by potential buyers. The wrong improvement, or the right improvement poorly executed, can even bring down the market value of a home. The suburban home that looks like a turreted castle may fill the heart of its owner/remodeler with joy, but the real estate agent who attempts to sell the property at a price that reflects its cost to the owner will have a frustrating task.

The "wrong" improvement (in terms of contribution to market value) isn't necessarily one of major proportions. Even a fireplace addition, which might ordinarily be a dollar-for-dollar contribution in some communities, can be overdesigned or overbuilt far out of proportion to the needs of the typical homeowner. Home remodelers are notorious for changing their minds after a project is under way, without realizing the impact any change can have on construction estimates. The "simple" substitution of imported marble with brass inserts for common used brick can have a significant effect on both material and labor costs.

Law of Increasing Returns and Law of Decreasing Returns

It is possible to overimprove a property. This happens when so many property improvements have been made, they no longer have a positive effect on value. As long as property improvements create a proportionate or greater increase in value, the **law of increasing returns** is in effect. When additional improvements no longer bring a corresponding increase in value, the **law of decreasing returns** is in effect.

Every neighborhood has at least one example of the "tinkerer." This is the homeowner who can't stop working on his or her home. After the bathroom skylight is installed, it's time to redecorate the living room or remodel the kitchen. When the inside work is finished (temporarily), it's time to regrade the lawn and add a new deck or gazebo. Up to a certain point, all of these improvements can add value to a house. If the property is a real "fixer-upper," the law of decreasing returns may not kick in for quite some time. Eventually, however, the home will be improved beyond the needs and financial capabilities of typical buyers in the market area.

EXAMPLE: Life in the Fast Lane

Sellers often have unrealistic expectations of what their property is worth. Let's consider an example in light of the value principles you have just read in this chapter.

Cathy Clark is selling her one-bedroom, one-bath condominium in a western suburb of Chicago, Illinois. She purchased the condo in 1987 for $42,000. Since then, she has taken great pains to redecorate each room in great taste, applying expensive wallpaper herself and sanding and refinishing the woodwork and floors. Because her company is moving its headquarters to a far western suburb, Cathy plans to sell her condo and purchase a small detached house in a new subdivision in McHenry County. In fact, she already has made a deposit on a model she particularly likes. Cathy gathers all her receipts for materials she used in remodeling her condo, computes a reasonable charge per hour for her labor and adds the total to her purchase price. She then factors in ten percent appreciation for each year she has owned the condo, based on an article about price appreciation in the Midwest that she read recently in a national newsmagazine. Finally, she subtracts her purchase price and costs from her estimated appreciated value to determine what her net profit from a sale should be. Her figures look like this:

Purchase Price		$42,000
Materials		
Wallpaper—30 rolls @ $50	$1,500	
Sandpaper	17	
Rental of sander	75	
Varnish	82	
Miscellaneous—wallpaper		
paste, brushes, clean up	63	
Labor—105 hours @ $10	1,050	
	$2,787	
Total Investment		44,787
After Appreciation for Four Years @ 10 percent		65,573
Net Profit ($65,573–$44,787)		$20,786

Cathy is very pleased with the results of her calculations and immediately makes an appointment with a nearby real estate broker to discuss listing her property for sale. The broker comes over that evening and begins his presentation. Cathy is a bit restless as the broker discusses the services his company can make available to her. She is puzzled when the broker mentions that he has brought along statistics on recent sales and listings of other condominiums in the area. Cathy is not very happy at all while the broker patiently explains to her why his competitive market analysis indicates that her condominium should bring a sales price somewhere in the $47,000 to $52,000 range.

In this example, Cathy Clark made several assumptions that many homeowners make when they try to value their properties themselves.

1. Cathy assumed that every dollar she invested in improvements to her property—both in materials and time (her labor)—resulted in a dollar-for-dollar increase in the property's value. She never heard of either the principle of contribution or the law of decreasing returns.
2. Cathy assumed that the rate of appreciation on her property has been the same as the overall rate of appreciation of all real estate in the area. She never heard of the principle of substitution or the principle of supply and demand. She has no inkling that externalities can impact her property's value. Because she is not "in" real estate, she has no interest in the number of other properties similar to her own that would be her competition in the marketplace. On top of everything else, Cathy's condo is in an older building that needs a new roof and tuckpointing, and several brand new condominium

developments are available in the area at below-market interest rates.

If you were in Cathy's place, you might not be happy with the sales prospects related to you by the real estate agent, but at least you would have some idea of the economic principles behind the agent's analysis.

The Appraisal Worksheet can be used to analyze a home and its neighborhood in terms of some of the valuation principles that have been considered in this chapter.

APPRAISAL WORKSHEET

Is the present use of the property its highest and best use? _____

In general, is the home in better condition, about the same condition or worse condition than others in the neighborhood? *Explain.*

_____

_____

Does the home conform to others in the neighborhood—	Yes	No
in age?	_____	_____
in lot size?	_____	_____
in home size?	_____	_____
in method and quality of construction?	_____	_____
in architectural style?	_____	_____
in interior layout?	_____	_____
in kind and maturity of landscaping?	_____	_____
in outdoor amenities, such as a deck or pool?	_____	_____

How old is the neighborhood? _____

Is the neighborhood in the stage of growth, in the stage of equilibrium or in the stage of decline? _____

What improvements have been made to the home?

_____

_____

Do you think the home is worth more now than when purchased? *Explain.*

_____

_____

3

The Appraisal Process

The basic problem when buying or selling real estate is deciding what it is worth. To derive a final estimate of value, the appraiser uses three traditional appraisal methods—the sales comparison approach, the cost approach and the income approach.

This chapter focuses on the basic definition of each of the value approaches. Also covered are the steps involved in the appraisal process, from an appraisal assignment through the final estimate of value.

SALES COMPARISON APPROACH

In the sales comparison approach, an estimate of value is obtained by comparing the property being appraised—the **subject property**—to recent sales of similar, nearby properties, called **comparables** or **comps.** The theory is that the value of the subject property is directly related to the sales prices of the comparable properties.

The objective of the sales comparison approach is to estimate the market value of the subject property. As stated previously, *market value* is the most probable price a property should bring in a sale occurring under normal market conditions—an arm's-length transaction. The market value estimate is based on actual sales of comparable properties. The appraiser must collect, classify, analyze and interpret a body of market data.

The rationale of the sales comparison approach is that a knowledgeable buyer will not pay more for a property than the cost to acquire a comparable alternative property (principle of substitution).

To implement the sales comparison approach, the appraiser finds three to five or more properties that have been sold recently and are similar to the subject property. The appraiser notes any dissimilar features and makes an adjustment for each by using the following formula:

$$\frac{\text{Sales Price of}}{\text{Comparable Property}} \pm \text{Adjustments} = \frac{\text{Indicated Value of}}{\text{Subject Property}}$$

Adjustments are made to the sales price of a comparable property by *adding* the value of features present in the subject property, but not in the comparable property and *subtracting* the value of features present in the comparable property but not in the subject property.

The adjusted sales prices of the comparables represent the probable value range of the subject property. From this range, a single market value estimate can be selected.

Major types of adjustments include those made for physical (on-site) features, locational (off-site) influences, conditions of the sale (buyer-seller motivation and financing terms) and the time from the date of the sale.

Here's a rule to remember when making adjustments:

A comparable property is always adjusted (either + or –)
to make it as similar to the subject property as possible.

This means that a property that has characteristics *more* valuable than the subject must be adjusted *downward*. A property that has characteristics *less* valuable than the subject must be adjusted *upward*. Let's see how this works.

EXAMPLE:

- House A, the subject property, has central air conditioning and a garage.
- A comparable property, house B, sold for $100,000 one month before the time of the appraisal. House B has a garage but no central air-conditioning, which is valued at $3,000.
- House C is comparable to the subject and sold recently for $95,000. House C has central air-conditioning but no garage, which is valued at $7,000.
- House D, also comparable to the subject property, sold recently for $114,000. It has both a garage and central air-conditioning. House D, however, is located in a better area of the neighborhood than the subject is. The location adjustment is valued at $10,000.

A summary of the adjustment information is as follows:

Comparable Sales Chart

	Comparables		
	B	C	D
Sales price	$100,000	$95,000	$114,000
Location			−10,000
Garage		+7,000	
Air-conditioning	+3,000		
Adjusted sales price	$103,000	$102,000	$104,000

The value of House A, the subject property, will fall within the price range of the adjusted comparable properties, that is, between $102,000 and $104,000. Large differences in value might suggest that the properties are not similar enough. In such cases, the appraiser would have to recheck the characteristics of the comparable properties and the validity of the sales.

The accuracy of an appraisal using the sales comparison approach depends on the appraiser's use of reliable adjustment values. How to determine these values and adjust for property differences is explained more fully in Chapter 6, which is devoted to the sales comparison approach.

COST APPROACH

Using the cost approach, the appraiser estimates the present reproduction cost of the house plus any other improvements to the land (such as a garage or patio) as if they were *new*. The appraiser then subtracts any loss in value caused by the *depreciation* of the improvements. **Depreciation** includes all of the influences that reduce the value of the subject house below its current reproduction cost.

Finally, the appraiser adds the estimated value of the site itself, usually found by analyzing sales of similar vacant sites.

The rationale of the cost approach is that a knowledgeable buyer will pay no more for a house than the cost of constructing a substitute house on a similar lot and in similar condition.

The formula for the cost approach is:

$$\text{Cost of Improvements New} - \text{Depreciation on Improvements} + \text{Site Value} = \text{Property Value}$$

Depreciation may occur through either *deterioration* or *obsolescence*. **Deterioration** is a loss in value to a home resulting from ordinary wear and tear, disintegration and exposure to the elements over time. The effects of deterioration may be a worn-out roof that needs new shingles, peeling paint, cracked windows and other physical deficiencies that make the property less desirable to potential buyers. **Obsolescence** can be *functional* or *external*. **Functional obsolescence** is a loss in value caused by deficiencies within the property, such as poor traffic patterns, outmoded room layout or design and inadequate mechanical equipment. **External obsolescence** is a loss in value caused by negative conditions outside the property, such as a lack of demand for properties in the neighborhood, changes in zoning or property uses in the area and the presence of nuisances and hazards such as excessive noise, smoke and traffic.

EXAMPLE:

The subject house is similar in size, design and quality of construction to a new house that cost $150,000 to build. The subject house has depreciated by ten percent due to normal wear and tear and is on a lot valued separately at $40,000. Using the cost approach formula:

$$\$150,000 - (.10 \times \$150,000) + \$40,000 = \text{Property Value}$$
$$\$150,000 - \$15,000 + \$40,000 = \$175,000$$

The estimated value of the subject property is $175,000.

INCOME APPROACH

The income approach is an analysis based on the relationship between the rate of return that an investor or buyer expects or requires and the net income that a property produces. This approach is used primarily for valuing income-producing properties such as apartment buildings, shopping centers and office buildings.

When applying the income approach to value, an appraiser must develop an operating statement for the property being appraised. This can be accomplished in five basic steps:

1. Estimate the potential gross income (rent plus all other income earned by the property);
2. Deduct an allowance for vacancies and collection losses (usually estimated as a percentage of potential gross income);
3. Calculate the amount of effective gross income (potential gross income less vacancy and collection losses);
4. Estimate the operating expenses; and
5. Deduct the expenses from the effective gross income to obtain the net operating income from the subject property.

Once a property's net operating income is known, the appraiser must develop the buyer's required rate of investment return. This rate of return is called the **capitalization rate** and is determined by comparing the relationship of the net operating income to the sales price of similar properties that have been sold in the current market.

Thus value can be computed by using this formula:

$$\frac{\text{Net Operating Income}}{\text{Capitalization Rate}} = \text{Property Value}$$

EXAMPLE:

A buyer requires a ten percent return on an apartment building that produces a net operating income of $50,000 per year. Applying the income approach formula, the property value is $50,000 ÷ .10, or $500,000.

Obviously, the income approach can be the most technically complex method of appraisal when applied to large income-producing properties. To perform such appraisals, an understanding of gross and net income streams, tax rules and capitalization techniques is essential. These concepts, however, are beyond the scope of this book. When appraising single-family homes, a far simpler method can be used as an alternative to the income approach. This method is based on the assumption that value is related to the *market rent* the property can be expected to earn.

Market rent is the rental income that a property would most probably command on the open market as indicated by current rentals paid for comparable space. To find the market rent, you must know what rent tenants have paid and are currently paying on comparable properties. By comparing present and past performances of properties similar to the subject, you should be able to determine the subject property's rent potential. By analyzing sales prices of comparable properties, you can determine the factor, or **gross rent multiplier (GRM),** that represents the relationship between market rent and market value. When the appropriate gross rent multiplier is applied to the rental income the subject property is expected to produce, the result is an estimate of market value. When appraising single-family residences, a rent multiplier is an accepted tool in the income approach to value.

Gross rent multipliers simply are numbers that express the relationship between the sales price of a residential property and its gross monthly unfurnished rental. This ratio can be expressed by this formula:

$$\frac{\text{Sales Price}}{\text{Gross Rent}} = \text{GRM}$$

To establish a reasonably accurate GRM, you should obtain recent sales and rental data from five or more properties similar to the subject that have sold in the same market area and were rented at the time of sale.

Figure 3.1 illustrates the calculation of a monthly gross rent multiplier.

FIGURE 3.1   Gross Rent Multiplier Calculation

Sale #	Sales Price	Monthly Rental	Gross Rent Multiplier
1	$90,000	$750	120.00
2	85,000	690	123.19
3	87,000	715	121.68
4	95,000	800	118.75
5	89,000	730	121.92
		Average =	121.11

Based on this marketing analysis, the appraiser probably would use 121 as the gross rent multiplier.

The estimated GRM then can be applied to the projected rental of the subject property to estimate its market value. The formula for this step is:

$$\text{Gross Rent} \times \text{GRM} = \text{Market Value}$$

EXAMPLE:

An appraiser has determined that the market rent for the subject property is $700 per month. The range of GRMs derived from recent sales of comparable properties is from 110 to 114. The appraiser concludes that the subject property's GRM should be 112. Using the GRM formula:

$700 $\times$ 112 = $78,400, the estimated value of the subject property using the gross rent multiplier method.

RELATIONSHIP OF APPROACHES

All three approaches to value are market oriented and must reflect market data and the market behavior of buyers (and builders, in the case of the cost approach).

Using the sales comparison approach, the subject property is compared with other similar properties recently sold, and adjustments are made for any differences. The prices at which properties sell in the market indicate the reactions of typical investors and users.

The income approach analyzes market-determined rents and expenses. The approach is based on the assumption that an investor in income property expects a certain return on the investment. It is on the basis of this return that he or she decides what to buy and how much to pay. For single-family houses, gross monthly rental is used and the ratio derived is called the gross rent multiplier.

With the cost approach, an estimate of value is obtained by adding land value to estimated reproduction cost new, less depreciation of the improvements. Land value is estimated by comparing the subject land with similar land recently sold in the market. Features of vacant land might include installation of utilities, composition of soil, terrain, shape, zoning and favorable location.

All the elements of cost are market phenomena, as are all types of depreciation. The estimate of reproduction cost new, for example, must be based on current labor rates and material costs. Physical deterioration is measured by the cost of labor and materials needed to cure it. Functional and external obsolescence are measured by the behavior of typical buyers, for their reactions to style, function, utility of buildings and the like give a reliable indication of the amount of loss incurred.

As a general rule, the sales comparison approach is most useful when appraising single-family homes. The cost approach is best applied to appraising non–income-producing property such as museums, libraries, churches, schools and other institutional buildings where there is no income and few sales, if any. The income approach is most useful when appraising investment property.

For any appraisal assignment, all three approaches can and should be used whenever possible. If nothing else, each approach serves as a check against the others. Keep in mind, however, that each approach must be based on verified market data.

STEPS IN THE APPRAISAL PROCESS

The flowchart in Figure 3.2 outlines the steps by which an appraisal is carried out. The basic process generally is the same, regardless of the purpose of the appraisal and the type of property being appraised.

1. *State the problem.* The appraiser begins by identifying the subject property—by its mailing address and by its more precise legal description, which can be found on an existing deed, mortgage instrument, title policy or various other public records.

   The appraiser then must note what the appraisal is to accomplish. Most often, the appraisal will be conducted to determine the market value for a prospective sale or loan. Once the objectives or goals of the appraisal are known, the approach(es) best suited to the subject property can be selected. All three basic approaches are traditionally used by appraisers whenever possible. Each method serves as a check against the others and narrows the range within which the final estimate of value will fall. Occasionally, only one

FIGURE 3.2   The Appraisal Process

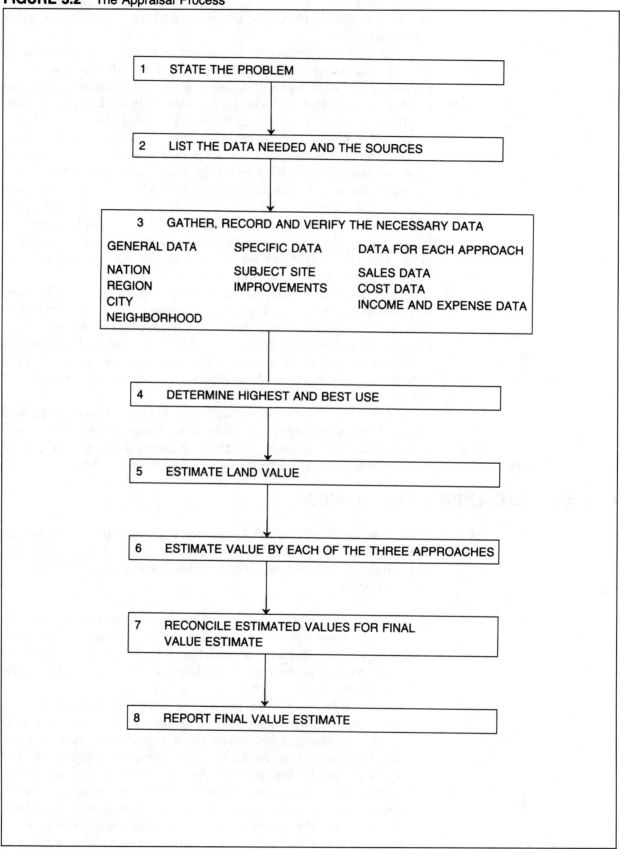

approach will be appropriate, because only a limited amount of data will be available for some properties.

2. *List the data needed and all the sources.* Based on the value approaches to be used, the appraiser determines the kinds of data that must be collected and the sources of that data.

3. *Gather, record and verify the necessary data.* Five categories of data are needed to make a reliable estimate of value:

   - General data on the geographic and economic features of the nation, region, city and neighborhood;
   - Specific data on the subject site and improvements—including a detailed physical description;
   - Sales data on comparable properties—to apply the sales comparison approach;
   - Cost data on construction of a like property plus accrued depreciation data on the subject property—to apply the cost approach; and
   - Sales and income data from properties similar to the subject that have been sold in the same market area and were rented at the time of the sale—to apply the gross rent multiplier method, a form of income approach for residential properties.

   The type of property being appraised will dictate the kinds of data that must be collected.

4. *Determine highest and best use.* The appraiser analyzes and interprets the market forces that influence the subject property to determine the property's most profitable use on which to base the final value estimate. For most residential subdivision developments, the current use of the property is its highest and best use.

5. *Estimate land value.* The location and improvements of the subject site (except for structures) are compared to those of similar nearby sites that have been sold recently. Adjustments are made for significant differences. The adjusted prices of the properties most like the subject are used to estimate the value of the subject site.

6. *Estimate value by each of the three approaches.* Using the sales comparison approach, the sales prices of recently sold comparable properties are adjusted to derive an estimate of value for the subject property. With the cost approach, the cost of property improvements less depreciation on improvements is added to the site value. Applying the income approach, value is based on the rental income the property is capable of earning, and in the simplest application of the income approach, a gross rent multiplier is derived.

7. *Reconcile the estimated values for the final value estimate.* All information must be reconciled or correlated and conclusions drawn from the collected facts. The appraiser never simply averages differing value estimates. The most relevant approach,

based on analysis and judgment, receives the greatest weight when determining the market value of the subject property.

8. *Report the final value estimate.* The appraiser's conclusion of value is presented in the form requested by the client. The report should include a summary of the data analyzed, the methods used and the reasoning that led to the appraiser's value estimate.

SUMMARY

The sales comparison approach is probably the best method for finding the fair market value of a house. The income approach is the least reliable, while the cost approach requires up-to-date information on current construction costs as well as intricate methods of depreciating older houses. Regardless of what approach is used, however, one must remember that the results are only estimates. The fair market value of any house also is greatly influenced by what the owner is willing to sell it for and by what the buyer is willing to pay for it. This final agreed-on price is, for all practical purposes, the value of the property.

The appraisal process begins with a statement of the problem, that is, the purpose of the appraisal. By gathering, recording and verifying all the necessary data, then analyzing and interpreting that information, the appraiser can form an opinion of value based on knowledge and understanding and not on guesswork.

In the Appraisal Worksheet that follows is a list of questions to help you gather some preliminary facts about the market picture in a neighborhood. You can find the answers to these questions by talking to local real estate agents, builders and, perhaps, even the people who publish the local newspaper.

APPRAISAL WORKSHEET

1. Is the population in the area growing? Declining? Holding steady? _____

2. How many new houses are for sale and how fast are they selling? _____

3. How many used houses are for sale and how fast are they selling? _____

4. What kinds of houses are selling best and why? _____

   _____

5. What kinds of houses aren't selling well? Why? _____

   _____

6. How great is the demand for rental housing? _____

7. What do homes rent for per month?   range _____

8. Is there a standard gross rent multiplier used in the area? _____
   If so, what is it? _____

9. What locations in the area are selling well? _____

   _____

10. What special features are liked and disliked by house hunters? _____

    _____

11. What is the cost per square foot for homes in the area? _____

12. What is the price range of homes sold in each market?

    New   _____

    Used   _____

    Rental _____

4

Data Collection and the Data Bank

At every step in the appraisal process, an appraiser will make use of data that has been diligently collected and carefully analyzed for its applicability to the property being appraised. The kinds of data the apprasier collects and considers are discussed in this chapter. Even though you may not have the resources of a professional appraiser, you should be able to find at least some of the data that will be mentioned. The more data you can find and interpret, the better you will understand the economic forces that affect property value.

THE APPRAISAL PROCESS

The last chapter covered the steps in the appraisal process, which are illustrated in the flowchart that appears on page 28. As the chart indicates, a considerable amount of data must be collected to make an accurate estimate of value. The appraiser will need:

- General data on the nation, region, city and neighborhood;
- Specific data on the subject site and improvements;
- Sales data for the sales comparison approach;
- Cost and depreciation data for the cost approach; and
- Income and expense data for the income approach.

The appraiser also must keep in mind the type of property being appraised. Certain data will be more important for some types of property and thus will receive more emphasis in the appraiser's research. Sales data on recent sales of comparable properties will be especially important when appraising a single-family residence, for example. Income and expense data will be of greatest importance when appraising an investment property, such as an apartment or office building. For special-purpose properties, such as school buildings, data on building costs tends to be most important.

THE DATA BANK

Figure 4.1 is the Data Bank. You will be referring to it throughout the rest of this book to help you determine the types of information required for an appraisal and where the information can be found.

The Source List

The first part of the Data Bank lists the typical sources that supply the information required for a real estate appraisal. Not every source listed may be available to you, and there may be other sources not on the list that are unique to your community. You can add to the list in the spaces numbered 45 through 50.

FIGURE 4.1   Data Bank

Data Source List

1. Personal inspection
2. Seller
3. Buyer
4. Broker
5. Salesperson
6. Neighbors
7. County register of deeds
8. Recorded mortgages and other financing instruments
9. Title reports
10. Transfer maps or books
11. Recorded subdivision plat maps
12. Area maps (topographic, soil)
13. Recorded leases
14. Banks, savings and loans and other lending institutions
15. City hall or county courthouse
16. Assessor's office
17. Published information on transfers, leases or assessed valuation
18. Local chamber of commerce
19. Property managers or owners
20. Building and architectural plans
21. Accountants
22. Financial statements
23. Building architects, contractors and engineers
24. County or city engineering commission
25. Regional or county government officials

26. Area planning commissions
27. Highway commissioner's office, road commission
28. Newspaper advertisements
29. Multiple-listing systems
30. Cost manuals (state, local, private)
31. Local material suppliers
32. Public utility companies
33. United States Bureau of the Census
34. Department of Commerce
35. Federal Housing Administration
36. Government councils
37. Local board of REALTORS®
38. National, state or local association of home builders
39. Public transportation officials
40. Professional journals
41. Railroad and transit authorities or companies
42. Labor organizations
43. Employment agencies
44. Airlines and bus lines, moving companies
45.
46.
47.
48.
49.
50.

FIGURE 4.1 Data Bank (Continued)

A. Regional Data

Types of Information	Sources
Topography	12
Natural resources	18, 12
Climate	18
Public transportation:	
Air	18, 44
Rail	18, 41
Expressways	27, 12
Population trends	26, 33, 36
Political organization and policies	25
Employment level	36, 42
Level of business activity and growth	14, 18
Average family income	26, 18
New building (amount and kind)	34
Percentage of home ownership	33
Electrical power consumption and new hookups	32

B. City Data

Types of Information	Sources
Topography	1, 12
Natural resources	1, 12
Climate	18
Public transportation:	
Air	18, 44
Rail	41, 44
Bus	39, 44
Subway	39, 44
Expressways	27, 12
Traffic patterns	15, 24, 27
Population trends	26, 33, 36
Family size	26
Zoning	15, 26
Building codes	15, 23, 24
Political organization, policies and personnel	15
Employment level	18, 36, 42
Professions, trades or skills required	18
Level of business activity and growth	14, 18
Average family income	18, 26
Rental rates	19, 37
Percentage of vacancies	4, 35, 37
New building (amount and kind)	19, 37, 38
Building permits issued	15, 24
Bank deposits and loans	14, 18
Percentage of home ownership	4, 33, 37
Tax structure	15, 16
Electrical power consumption and new hookups	32

FIGURE 4.1   Data Bank (Continued)

C.   Neighborhood Data

Types of Information	Sources
Topography	1, 12
Boundaries	1, 4, 15, 11
Public transportation:	
Bus	39
Subway	39
Frequency of service	39
Distance to boarding point	1, 39
Distance and time to reach central business district	1, 39
Traffic patterns	1, 26, 36, 39
Family size	4, 26
Population density	18, 26
Population trend	18, 36
Zoning, codes or regulations	15, 24, 26
Employment level	4, 14, 18
Professions and trades	4, 6, 18
Average family income	33, 34, 18, 42
Percentage of home ownership	14, 37, 33
Level of business activity and growth	14, 18
New building (amount and kind)	23, 31
Building permits issued	15, 24
Taxes and assessments	15, 16
Utilities or improvements available (streets, curbs, sidewalks; water; electricity; telephone; gas; sewers)	15, 32
Percent built up	15, 37
Predominant type of building	1, 16, 19, 23
Typical age of buildings	1, 16, 19, 23
Condition of buildings	1, 26, 36, 31
Price range of typical properties	4, 9, 35, 37
Marketability	4, 37
Life cycle	1, 4
Land value trend	4, 16, 37
Location of facilities:	
Churches	1, 26, 12
Schools	1, 26, 44
Shopping	1, 26, 44
Recreational, cultural	1, 26, 44
Avenues of approach	1, 24
Types of services offered	32
Availability of personnel	26, 18
Employee amenities (shopping, eating and banking facilities)	1
Marketing area	26, 18
Competition	1, 18
Types of industry (light, heavy)	18
Sources of raw materials	18
Hazards and nuisances	1, 6, 25
Deed restrictions	7, 9
Changing use of area	4, 18

FIGURE 4.1 Data Bank (Continued)

D. Site Data

Types of Information	Sources
Legal description	7
Dimensions and area	1, 7, 11
Street frontage	1, 7, 11
Location in block	7, 11
Topography	7, 12
Topsoil and drainage	23, 12
Landscaping	1
Improvements:	
Streets, curbs, sidewalks	1, 15, 24
Water	32
Electricity	32
Telephone	32
Gas	32
Sewers	1, 15, 24
Tax rates and assessed valuation	16
Liens and special assessments	9, 16
Zoning, codes or regulations	16, 26
Easements and encroachments	1, 7, 9
Status of title	9

E. Building Data

Types of Information	Sources
Architectural style	1, 23
Date of construction and additions	7, 16, 24
Placement of building on land	1, 24, 12
Dimensions and floor area	20, 11
Floor plan(s)	20, 24
Construction materials used (exterior and interior)	20, 23, 31
Utilities available	1, 32, 18
Interior utility and other installations:	1, 16, 20
Heating and air-conditioning	
Plumbing	
Wiring	
Special equipment, such as elevators	
Exceptions to zoning, codes or regulations	7, 24, 26
Status of title	9
Mortgages and liens	7, 14
Condition of building	1, 16, 26

F. Sales Data

Types of Information	Sources
Date of sale	1 to 7, 29
Sales price	1 to 7, 29
Name of buyer and seller	1 to 7, 29
Deed book and page	7, 10
Reasons for sale and purchase	2 to 5

FIGURE 4.1   Data Bank (Continued)

G.   Cost Data

Types of Information	Sources
Building reproduction cost	23, 30, 31, 42
Building replacement cost	23, 30, 31, 42
Depreciation factors:	
Physical deterioration	1, 23, 30
Functional obsolescence	1, 20, 23, 30
External obsolescence	1, 23, 26, 30

H.   Income and Expense Data

Types of Information	Sources
Income data (both subject and comparable properties):	
Annual income	22
Current lease terms	1, 19
Occupancy history	19, 22
Collection loss history	19, 22
Fixed expense data (both subject and comparable properties):	16, 19, 22, 40
Real estate taxes	
Insurance	
Operating expense data (both subject and comparable properties):	16, 19, 22, 40
Management	
Payroll	
Legal and accounting	
Maintenance	
Repairs	
Supplies	
Painting and decorating	
Fuel	
Electricity	
Miscellaneous	
Reserves for replacement	1, 22, 30

Types of Data Needed

The Data Bank also contains eight lists that indicate the most appropriate sources for the various types of data necessary at every step in the appraisal process. Each type of listed information is keyed to one or more of the 44 sources of information itemized in the source list. You can add references to any other sources that you have found useful. Here's how the Data Bank works.

EXAMPLE:

A new subdivision is being built not far from your home. During a Sunday drive, you notice that construction work has begun along both sides of the roadway, but no workers are present that you can question. How can you find out what kind of work is under way?

In Data Bank List D, "Site Data," you look up "Improvements" and find four possible sources of information—source list numbers 1, 15, 24 and 32. The sources are (1) personal inspection, (15) city hall or county courthouse, (24) county or city engineering commission and (32) public utility companies. Because you already have inspected the property personally, you would contact the other sources, the most pertinent one first. In this case, the county or city engineering commission probably could tell you the reason for the construction activity. The department that issues building permits should have the information that you want.

DATA FORMS

As with any other project that requires the collection of a great deal of information, using well-drafted forms can help an appraisal proceed much more smoothly, efficiently and accurately. Completing data collection forms can help ensure that no details of the property, its location or the information required for each of the three appraisal techniques are overlooked.

The rest of this chapter includes forms that can be used to collect and record data on the neighborhood, site and building that are the subject of an appraisal. These are the types of information that will be most readily available to you and are the easiest to understand. A professional appraiser also would have considerable information on the region and city and would have to update that information frequently. Part of an appraiser's job is to keep up to date on economic indicators such as employment level and business starts (or failures), as well as political trends that could signal governmental policy changes affecting property values. The more aware you make yourself of wider economic influences, the better you will be able to identify and understand the factors that affect the value of a property.

Neighborhood Data Form

A Neighborhood Data Form such as the one shown in Figure 4.2 can help an appraiser gather some of the basic information needed for an appraisal report. An appraiser who makes many appraisals in the same area probably would not have to complete a new Neighborhood Data Form for each appraisal. The appraiser would have to update the form as often as necessary, perhaps only every year or so, or more often, as current economic conditions dictated.

Although Data Bank List C, "Neighborhood Data," supplies sources for much of the needed neighborhood information, a considerable amount of fieldwork still is necessary. The appraiser

FIGURE 4.2   Neighborhood Data Form

NEIGHBORHOOD DATA FORM

BOUNDARIES: ADJACENT TO:

    NORTH _____   _____

    SOUTH _____   _____

    EAST _____   _____

    WEST _____   _____

TOPOGRAPHY: _____ ☐ URBAN ☐ SUBURBAN ☐ RURAL

STAGE OF LIFE CYCLE OF NEIGHBORHOOD: ☐ GROWTH ☐ EQUILIBRIUM ☐ DECLINE

% BUILT UP: _____ GROWTH RATE: ☐ RAPID ☐ SLOW ☐ STEADY

AVERAGE MARKETING TIME: _____ PROPERTY VALUES: ☐ INCREASING ☐ DECREASING ☐ STABLE

SUPPLY/DEMAND: ☐ OVERSUPPLY ☐ UNDERSUPPLY ☐ BALANCED

CHANGE IN PRESENT LAND USE: _____

POPULATION: ☐ INCREASING ☐ DECREASING ☐ STABLE   AVERAGE FAMILY SIZE: _____

AVERAGE FAMILY INCOME: _____ INCOME LEVEL: ☐ INCREASING ☐ DECREASING

PREDOMINANT OCCUPATIONS: _____

TYPICAL PROPERTIES:	% OF	AGE	PRICE RANGE	% OWNER OCCUPIED	% RENTALS
VACANT LOTS					
SINGLE-FAMILY RESIDENCES					
2–6-UNIT APARTMENTS					
OVER 6-UNIT APARTMENTS					
NONRESIDENTIAL PROPERTIES					

TAX RATE: _____ ☐ HIGHER ☐ LOWER ☐ SAME AS COMPETING AREAS

SPECIAL ASSESSMENTS OUTSTANDING: _____ EXPECTED: _____

SERVICES: ☐ POLICE ☐ FIRE ☐ GARBAGE COLLECTION   OTHER: _____

DISTANCE AND DIRECTION FROM

    BUSINESS AREA: _____

    COMMERCIAL AREA: _____

    PUBLIC ELEMENTARY AND HIGH SCHOOLS: _____

    PRIVATE ELEMENTARY AND HIGH SCHOOLS: _____

    RECREATIONAL AND CULTURAL AREAS: _____

    CHURCHES AND SYNAGOGUES: _____

    EXPRESSWAY INTERCHANGE: _____

    PUBLIC TRANSPORTATION: _____

        TIME TO REACH BUSINESS AREA: _____ COMMERCIAL AREA: _____

    EMERGENCY MEDICAL SERVICE: _____

GENERAL TRAFFIC CONDITIONS: _____

PROXIMITY TO HAZARDS (AIRPORT, CHEMICAL STORAGE, ETC.): _____

PROXIMITY TO NUISANCES (SMOKE, NOISE, ETC.): _____

must note the general condition of all the houses in the area, as well as their size, the quality of landscaping and the degree of architectural conformity present. These and other factors will help the appraiser determine whether the neighborhood is likely to retain its appearance and value or decline in value.

Most of the categories of information required to complete the Neighborhood Data Form are self-explanatory, but some warrant further explanation.

Neighborhood Boundaries

In some newer subdivisions, neighborhood boundaries are conspicuously established by a gated entry and walled perimeter. Other neighborhoods, particularly those in older cities, are set off by other factors. These can include:

1. Natural boundaries (actual physical barriers—ravines, lakes, rivers and highways or other major traffic arteries);
2. Differences in land use (changes in zoning from residential to commercial or parkland);
3. Average value or age of homes; and
4. Income level of residents.

When filling out the Neighborhood Data Form, the appraiser records the street name or other identifiable dividing line and notes the type of property adjacent to the subject neighborhood at that boundary. A residential property adjacent to a park usually will have a higher value than a similar property adjacent to a railroad yard, for instance.

Stage of Life Cycle

A typical neighborhood usually goes through three distinct periods in its life: **growth, equilibrium** and **decline.**

Residential property values tend to increase during the period in which an area is first developed. When few vacant building sites remain, the houses in the neighborhood generally reach equilibrium at their highest monetary value, and prices will rarely fluctuate downward. As the years go by, however, and the effects of property deterioration become visible, the area usually will decline both in desirability and value. The process of decline can be accelerated by many factors, which may include:

- The availability of new housing nearby;
- Successive ownership of homes by lower-income residents who may not be able to afford the increasing maintenance costs of older homes; and
- Conversion of some properties to rental units, which may not be properly maintained.

As properties decrease in value, some may even be put to a different use, such as light industry, which, in turn, further decreases the attractiveness of the surrounding neighborhood for residential use. The life cycle is not always downward, however. It may begin an upswing because of **revitalization** if demand increases and provides the economic stimulus needed for neighborhood renovation. This process has occurred in many cities where the high demand for housing and the desire to avoid a long commute has prompted buyer interest in older homes that offer convenience of location as well as, in some cases, architectural distinctiveness. The **gentrification** of an urban neighborhood can be both a blessing to property owners and yet a curse to other residents and business people. Renters and merchants may find themselves priced out of their once inexpensive lodgings and establishments as increasing property values prompt higher rental rates.

In general, the classic life-cycle pattern previously described is the result of an overall economic growth coupled with an increasing consumer demand and the availability of land for housing and commercial development. In recent years, this pattern has been subjected to volatile market conditions.

During the 1970s, high interest rates and a prolonged period of economic recession combined with limited land availability to make property ownership increasingly expensive. As a result, the dream of home ownership was placed beyond the means of many more people than it formerly was. Existing housing became much more desirable and, for many, making repairs and improvements to an older building became a viable alternative to buying a new home. In response to this slowing of residential life cycles and the demand for tax-sheltered investments, developers concentrated on commercial structures, such as office buildings, overbuilding many desirable urban and suburban areas.

The 1980s brought a much lower rate of inflation, declining interest rates and indicators of a general economic recovery that helped revive the sluggish real estate housing market. The number of new building starts rose as demand increased, and the pace of development helped compensate for the slower preceding years. The Tax Reform Act of 1986 greatly limited the use of real estate as a tax shelter, but that limitation has emphasized the necessity for prudent investment. A competent appraisal is one of the ways in which the soundness of an investment can be determined.

The country entered the 1990s in a period of overall recession, yet housing costs still represented a significantly greater proportion of living expenses than was true even a decade earlier. Even though housing prices have continued to stagnate or decline in many areas, overall demand prompted by the great wave of home-buying baby boomers has reduced the level of home affordability and thus ownership to record lows. The 1990 census indicated a drop in home ownership over the past decade, for the first time since the 1930s. Overall, home ownership dropped from 66 percent of U.S. households in 1980 to 64 percent in 1989. Although the rate of home ownership actually increased among those 60 or older, it dropped for all other age groups, particularly those between 35 to 39.

Demand is not the only influence on property values, however. Social and political decisions by voters and government officials may accelerate or delay the factors that lead to a decline in sales prices. As the population grows, additional demand for housing is not being automatically met by new development. Financing for new construction has become much more of a hurdle for builders of both small and large developments. In some areas, housing growth now is deliberately limited for environmental or other reasons. When development to meet housing needs is limited, for whatever reasons, the state of equilibrium of existing housing may be much longer than would otherwise be the case. In other words, homeowners are more likely to repair or remodel their present housing when they can't afford to buy new housing elsewhere.

Knowledge of the existence of all of these factors and how they are interrelated is part of the appraiser's job. In short, the appraiser must be sensitive to all determinants of value, including economic, social and governmental influences, to gauge accurately these influences on neighborhood development.

Proximity to Hazards and Nuisances

We are becoming increasingly aware of the importance of the proximity of the neighborhood, or any part of it, to hazards or nuisances. The more we learn about environmental conditions, the more likely we are to discover factors that are injurious to health or safety. The mere potential for danger (such as chemical storage facilities) may lower property values in nearby areas. Active contamination may present an insurmountable barrier to marketability. One of the "worse case" examples of recent years has been the attempted rehabilitation of the Love Canal area of New York. Even after significant remediation efforts, it is questionable whether the majority of the homes that were vacated will ever be reoccupied.

The appraiser should be aware of any existing or potential hazard, as well as ones that have been alleviated.

Site Data Form

The Site Data Form shown in Figure 4.3 can be used to record the information needed to describe the subject site.

The appraiser begins by obtaining a complete and legally accurate description of the property's location and making a sketch to show the property's approximate shape and street location. A public building or other landmark also could be shown on the sketch to help locate the site. The topography (surface features) of

FIGURE 4.3 Site Data Form

SITE DATA FORM

ADDRESS: _____

LEGAL DESCRIPTION: _____

_____

_____

_____

_____

DIMENSIONS: _____

SHAPE: _____   SQUARE FEET: _____

TOPOGRAPHY: _____   VIEW: _____

NATURAL HAZARDS: _____

☐ INSIDE LOT   ☐ CORNER LOT   ☐ FRONTAGE: _____

ZONING: _____   ADJACENT AREAS: _____

UTILITIES: ☐ ELECTRICITY   ☐ GAS   ☐ WATER   ☐ TELEPHONE

☐ SANITARY SEWER   ☐ STORM SEWER

IMPROVEMENTS: DRIVEWAY: _____   STREET: _____

SIDEWALK: _____   CURB/GUTTER: _____   ALLEY: _____

STREETLIGHTS: _____

LANDSCAPING: _____

TOPSOIL: _____   DRAINAGE: _____

EASEMENTS: _____

DEED RESTRICTIONS: _____

SITE PLAT:

the site should be indicated, along with any natural hazards, such as a floodplain, earthquake fault zone or other potentially dangerous condition.

Other important features of the site are its size in square feet, location in terms of position in the block, utilities, improvements, soil composition and view. The historically higher value of a corner-lot location may not hold true in residential areas with lots 50 feet or more in width. Depending on the placement of the house on the site, the comparative privacy of the corner property may be offset by exposure to busy streets. The opposite would be true for a commercial site, however, where a high traffic count would be desirable.

Soil composition is always important. If the soil is unable to support a building, piles will have to be driven to carry the weight. On the other hand, bedrock within a few feet of the surface may require blasting before a suitable foundation can be established. In either case, the cost of preconstruction site preparation would decrease the site's value.

Knowledge of the subject site's zoning, which will affect its future use, is necessary, as is knowledge of the current zoning of the surrounding areas. A site zoned for a single-family residence may be poorly used for that purpose if the neighborhood is declining and multiunit buildings are being built nearby. In such a case, the feasibility of changing the zoning to multiunit residential construction might be analyzed by making a highest and best use study.

Finally, any easements or deed restrictions should be noted. Any part of the site that cannot be used for building purposes should be clearly designated, along with any other limitation on site use. Such limitations could raise or lower site value. An easement, for example, may allow airspace or below-ground space for present or future utility installations. Another kind of easement may give an adjoining property owner the right to travel over the property. Deed restrictions, usually set up by the property's subdivider, may specify the size of lots used for building, the type or style of building constructed, setbacks from property lines or other factors designed to increase the subdivision's homogeneity and thus stabilize property values.

Building Data Form

The Building Data Form shown in Figure 4.4 can be used to appraise a single-family residence. Not all categories of information will apply to every house, however. The appraiser can draw a line through any item that does not apply to a particular property.

Even before entering a single-family house, the appraiser is called on to make certain judgments.

Approaching the house from the street, the appraiser makes a note of the first impression created by the house, its orientation and how it fits in with the surrounding area. At the same time,

FIGURE 4.4   Building Data Form

BUILDING DATA FORM

ADDRESS: _____

NO. OF UNITS: _____   NO. OF STORIES: _____   ORIENTATION: N S E W

TYPE: _____   DESIGN: _____   AGE: _____   SQUARE FEET: _____

	GOOD	AVERAGE	FAIR	POOR
GENERAL CONDITION OF EXTERIOR				
FOUNDATION TYPE _____ BSMT./CRAWL SP./SLAB				
EXTERIOR WALLS: BRICK/BLOCK/VENEER/STUCCO/				
WOOD/ALUMINUM/VINYL				
WINDOW FRAMES: METAL/WOOD				
STORM WINDOWS: ____ SCREENS: ____				
GARAGE: _____ ATTACHED/DETACHED				
NUMBER OF CARS: ____				
☐ PORCH ☐ DECK ☐ PATIO ☐ SHED				
OTHER _____				
GENERAL CONDITION OF INTERIOR				
INTERIOR WALLS: DRY WALL/PLASTER/WOOD				
CEILINGS: _____				
FLOORS: WOOD/CONCRETE/TILE/CARPET				
ELECTRICAL WIRING AND SERVICE: _____				
HEATING PLANT: _____ AGE: _____				
GAS/OIL/WOOD/ELECTRIC				
CENTRAL AIR-CONDITIONING: _____ AIR FILTRATION: ___				
NUMBER OF FIREPLACES: _____ TYPE: _____				
OTHER _____				
BATHROOM: FLOOR___WALLS____FIXTURES _____				
BATHROOM: FLOOR___WALLS____FIXTURES _____				
BATHROOM: FLOOR___WALLS____FIXTURES _____				
KITCHEN: FLOOR___WALLS____CABINETS _____				
FIXTURES _____				

ROOM SIZES	LIVING ROOM	DINING ROOM	KITCHEN	BEDROOM	BATH	CLOSETS	FAMILY ROOM
BASEMENT							
1ST FLOOR							
2ND FLOOR							
ATTIC							

DEPRECIATION (DESCRIBE):

PHYSICAL DETERIORATION _____

FUNCTIONAL OBSOLESCENCE _____

EXTERNAL OBSOLESCENCE _____

the appraiser notes and records information about the landscaping. Next, the external construction materials (for the foundation, outside walls, roof, driveway, etc.) and the condition of each are listed and the general external condition of the building is rated. Finally, the appraiser measures each structure on the site, sketches its dimensions and computes its area in square feet.

Inside the house, the appraiser notes and evaluates major construction details and fixtures, particularly:

- Interior finish;
- Kind of floors, walls and doors;
- Condition and adequacy of kitchen cabinets;
- Type and condition of heating and air-conditioning systems;
- Rooms with special features, such as built-in bookcases and fireplaces; and
- All other features that indicate the quality of construction.

The appraiser also observes the general condition of the house for evidence of recent remodeling, cracked plaster, sagging floors or any other signs of deterioration, and records room dimensions and total square footage.

The appraiser then notes the general condition of the building, giving consideration to three kinds of depreciation:

1. *Physical deterioration.* The effects of ordinary wear and tear and the action of the elements.
2. *Functional obsolescence.* The inadequacy of features in the design, layout or construction of the building that are currently desired by purchasers, or the presence of features that have become unfashionable or unnecessary. Fixtures such as bathtubs or vanities also fall into this category. A kitchen without modern, built-in cabinets and sink would be undesirable in most areas.
3. *External obsolescence.* A feature made undesirable or unnecessary because of conditions outside the property. A change of zoning from residential to commercial might make a single-family house obsolete if such usage does not fully utilize (take full monetary advantage of) the site.

The kinds of depreciation and how each affects the value of the property are explained in greater detail in the chapters on the specific appraisal approaches. When the appraiser first records the building data, it is enough to make a general estimate of the degree of physical deterioration, functional obsolescence or external obsolescence present in the property.

An appraiser cannot determine some property features without actually taking the building apart. If all of the items on the Data Collection Form have been noted and recorded, however, the appraiser should be able to identify most of the building's deficiencies, as well as its special features. Information received only from the owner or from some other source and not personally verified by the appraiser can be recorded, but the source of the information should be supplied. For instance, the owner may know, or may have been told, that the house has wall, floor and ceiling insulation rated R-19 (a measure of insulation performance, explained further in the next chapter). If so, that information and its source should be noted.

As you read through the rest of this book, you will be filling out the forms presented in this chapter. Keep in mind that no standardized form can ever be perfectly suited to every type of property. Also, significant regional differences exist across the United States, in both building design and construction. Climatic requirements probably account for the greatest number of construction variables. The basement that is highly desirable in the Midwest or Northeast as a cold barrier and storage area may be an expensive oddity in the West or Southwest. Design is very often dictated by local tastes, influenced over the years by the availability of construction materials. The ground-hugging adobe house typical of the Santa Fe style would look out of place among the wood-sided homes of a New England village.

As you complete the Appraisal Worksheet that follows, be sure to record any distinct regional property characteristics that contribute to value. Also note any unusual property characteristics that may detract from value.

APPRAISAL WORKSHEET

1. What are the boundaries of the immediate neighborhood? _____
   _____

2. Categorize the neighborhood as urban, suburban or rural. _____
   _____

3. In what stage of the life cycle (growth, equilibrium or decline) is the neighborhood? ___

4. What is the average family income in the neighborhood? _____

5. What are typical occupations of its residents? _____

6. What percentage of properties in the neighborhood are single-family residences? _____
   2- to 6-unit apartment buildings? _____ larger apartment buildings? _____
   vacant lots? _____ nonresidential buildings? _____

7. What is the property tax rate? _____ How does it compare to the rate in nearby
   areas? _____

8. What special assessments must property owners pay, and how do these compare to
   assessments in other areas? _____
   _____

9. How far is the house from the business area, schools and other amenities? _____

10. Are there any hazards or nuisances in the neighborhood or nearby? _____ If so,
    identify them and their proximity to the house. _____

11. What is the legal description of the property?_____
    _____

12. What is the size, shape and topography of the lot? _____
    _____

13. What is the property's zoning classification? _____

14. Are there any easements across the property and, if so, what are they?_____
    _____

15. List any restrictions in the deed to the property. _____
    _____
    _____

16. Describe the design and general outside features of the house and the house's overall
    condition. _____
    _____
    _____

APPRAISAL WORKSHEET (Continued)

17. Describe the interior features of the house, including floor and wall coverings and kitchen cabinets, and note their condition. _____

_____

_____

_____

18. What kind of electrical service does the house have? _____

19. Describe the home's heating plant and air-conditioning or cooling system, if any. _____

_____

20. Note the number and size of the rooms in the house, as well as its total square footage. _____

_____

_____

5

Residential Construction and Home Inspection

To appraise a home, you first must check its neighborhood for livability and investment potential. Then you must analyze and evaluate its site. Finally, you must inspect the house itself and give an opinion about its condition. An appraiser must methodically check the house's interior design, the physical condition of its foundation, structural framework, interior and exterior surfaces and mechanical systems. Obviously, a basic understanding of construction is an extremely handy aptitude to possess. An appraiser must look beyond the visible charm and appeal of the house and view it with a cold objective attitude and with the trained eye of a detective. A person conducting an appraisal also must be able to ask questions and to find answers.

This chapter considers various factors of the neighborhood, lot and house that contribute to and detract from value and resale potential. It also covers the basics of new-home construction.

NEIGHBORHOOD

A **neighborhood** is an area within which any change has an immediate and direct influence on the value of the subject property. It is the starting point when gathering factual information for an appraisal.

A home should be viewed as an investment whose future value will be greatly influenced by the neighborhood's evolution. A location can be checked for livability and investment potential simply by touring the area. Without even talking to anyone, you can determine how people in a neighborhood feel about their homes. The total visual impression is a true indicator of the community's personality. Pride of ownership is reflected in the decorative features, fresh paint, flowers, well-kept lawns and so on. Older neighborhoods that have been well maintained probably will stay that way. Homeowners are likely to remain in these areas and continue to protect their investments.

On the other hand, indifference—a lack of caring—gives the impression of premature oldness to the neighborhood. When several homes appear neglected in what is otherwise a well-kept neighborhood, this may be an early sign that those homeowners are financially burdened or just don't care. If that situation continues, within a few years the property values in that area could level off or begin to decline.

Do the surrounding houses conform architecturally? Many houses lose value simply because they do not conform to their neighborhood. Too much conformity, on the other hand, where all the houses look the same, also will diminish value. Houses within a neighborhood should have enough variations in style and design to give a pleasing overall effect.

Are all homes in the area in the same general price range? The biggest, most expensive home on the block will not have the same resale value in a moderately priced neighborhood as it would if it were located in an area of comparable or higher-priced homes. As a rule of thumb, appraisers, mortgage lenders and other real estate professionals have found that the resale value of relatively inexpensive homes in a good area will be pulled up by higher-priced homes, while the value of large, expensive homes will be pulled down by surrounding lower-priced homes.

Environmental Hazards

The presence of environmental conditions such as smoke, fog, noxious fumes, radon contamination, asbestos-containing materials, urea-formaldehyde insulation and proximity to toxic waste dumps and old landfills not only threatens the health of neighborhood residents, but it also can have a significant negative effect on the value and marketability of property in the area.

The checklist in Figure 5.1 can be used to analyze and evaluate the neighborhood in which the subject property is located.

SITE

Site inspection begins with a survey of the grounds and the house from a distance to get an overall impression of the landscaping, driveway, walks, patios, decks, fences and other structures on the property. Keep in mind that, although it is rare to find a site landscaped and laid out to perfection, the grounds should be in reasonably good shape.

FIGURE 5.1   How Does the Neighborhood Rate?

		YES	NO
1.	Surrounding houses conform architecturally?	___	___
2.	Homes in the area in the same general price range?	___	___
3.	Homes well cared for?	___	___
4.	Lawns well kept?	___	___
5.	Adequate police and fire protection?	___	___
6.	All utilities available?	___	___
7.	Shopping, schools, churches, parks, medical facilities and recreation areas nearby?	___	___
8.	Convenient to place of employment?	___	___
9.	Owner occupied?	___	___
10.	Trash collection, snow removal and road maintenance available?	___	___
11.	Who lives there—ages, income, children, interests? _____		
12.	Access to public transportation?	___	___
13.	Taxes in line with competing areas?	___	___
14.	Special assessments?	___	___
15.	Property values rising?	___	___
16.	Good schools?	___	___
17.	Current or anticipated zoning restrictions?	___	___
18.	Radon contamination in the area?	___	___
19.	Good quality of water?	___	___
20.	Hazardous traffic patterns?	___	___
21.	Irritating noise levels from cars, trucks, airplanes, trains or buses?	___	___
22.	Adequate parking?	___	___
23.	Leash laws for pets?	___	___
24.	Street paving in good condition?	___	___
25.	Plans for expansion and development?	___	___

Orientation: Locating the House on the Site

The site should be an integral part of the design of a house. Correct siting on the property can make the house more pleasant to live in and more attractive to buyers when it is placed on the market. The site should be analyzed for its topography, the variations in the sun's path from season to season, the types and sizes of trees, the views, the noise and the proximity to neighbors. Once these factors are studied, the builder can properly orient the house to take full advantage of the site's special characteristics. For example, if the land is built up, the house should be located on the highest point so that rainwater drains away from the house.

When orienting a house for maximum natural light, builders should be aware that morning sun is from the east and evening sun from the west. Midday sun is from the south, and in winter the sun is far to the south, making it an excellent heat source.

The north side of the house receives no direct sunlight and may be a good location for bedrooms.

With good site planning, land is set aside and designed for three different functions: *public* use, *service* use and *private* use. The **public** space or zone is the area visible from the street—usually the land in front of the house—and concern should be taken about the impression it makes on people driving by or coming to the main entrance. Zoning regulations specify how far back a house must be placed on a lot. The **service** zone consists of the driveway, the walks and the areas where trash and garbage can be collected and outdoor equipment can be stored. It should be designed so that deliveries can be made to the service entrance without intrusion into space intended only for private use. The **private** zone is the outdoor living space for the family. It may include a patio, a deck and hot tub, a barbecue pit, a garden and a play area for children.

In most cases, a minimum amount of valuable land should be allocated for public and service use and the maximum amount for private enjoyment. Thus, architects prefer to situate a house near the street to provide a larger backyard.

Use the checklist in Figure 5.2 for an examination of the subject site.

FIGURE 5.2   Site Checklist

		YES	NO
1.	Does the site have all the necessary utilities?	_____	_____
2.	Is the site well landscaped?	_____	_____
3.	Does the landscaping provide privacy?	_____	_____
4.	Does the topography of the land allow for good drainage?	_____	_____
5.	Are the public, service and private zones of the site well defined?	_____	_____
6.	Have you checked on any easements or deed restrictions?	_____	_____
7.	Is the size of the site standard within the neighborhood?	_____	_____
8.	Does the house take good advantage of natural conditions (sun, breeze, view)?	_____	_____

Next is the house itself. Because most houses today are constructed with wood frames, this chapter will focus on the elements involved in the construction and design of wood-frame residences.

BUILDING CODES

The purpose of building codes is to ensure that builders follow minimum standards for construction. Different codes may be in effect in specific regions of the country. These include the Uniform Building Code, the National Electric Code and the Uniform Plumbing Code, plus any state and local codes. Some cities, for example, have new energy codes that require an entire house to conform to code if new rooms are added. In such a case, the builder may be required to install new windows throughout the house even if the homeowner is adding only a bedroom. The local building department can provide information on any such requirements.

PLANS AND SPECIFICATIONS

Detailed plans and specifications are required to comply with building codes. Working drawings, called **plans** or **blueprints,** show the construction details of the house, while **specifications** are written instructions that tell the builder what materials to use, where to use them and what results to expect.

ARCHITECTURAL STYLES

Although construction details are rigidly specified by building codes, house styles may vary greatly. No absolute standards exist, and real estate values rest on what potential buyers, users and investors think is desirable, as well as on what they consider to be attractive.

The outward appearance of a home may adhere to one style only or a combination of several different styles. A house shouldn't be a mishmash of details, however—a little something for everybody. Materials, scale and proportion must be consistent with the architectural style. For example, if windows are not properly placed and sized, there's always going to be something not quite right about the home's appearance. Colonial brick on a Spanish ranch is a waste of two good ideas. Over the years, a home that's true to its design will mature gracefully and always be in good taste. Figure 5.3 shows several house styles that have been popular for many years.

The architectural style of a home provides long-range appeal to users and investors. The factors that affect appeal are difficult to identify and differ according to style trends and individual preferences and tastes.

HOUSE TYPES

Although variations exist, most home types fall somewhere within the basic categories described as follows and as illustrated in Figure 5.4.

Ranch

This one-story structure with broad overhangs has all the habitable rooms on one level. Ranches are built low to the

FIGURE 5.3 House Styles

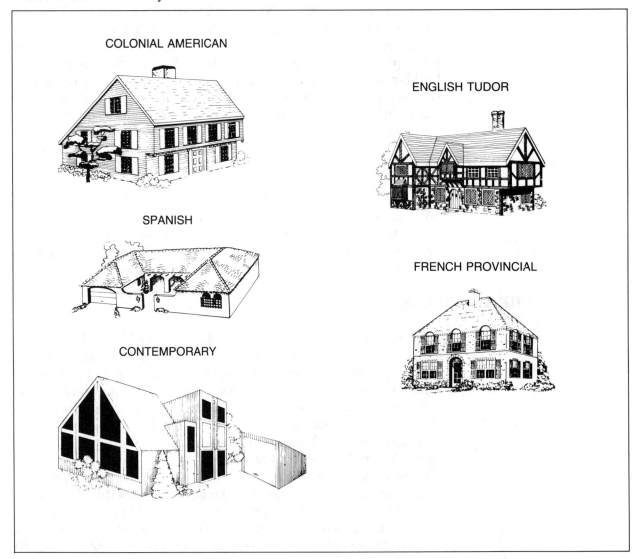

COLONIAL AMERICAN

ENGLISH TUDOR

SPANISH

FRENCH PROVINCIAL

CONTEMPORARY

ground, often with no more than two steps from the entry to the grade.

Raised Ranch

A ranch house with the basement area raised slightly out of the ground has two distinct levels and no entry between levels. Stairs from the outside usually lead up to the main-level living area.

Split Entry

Although this house type is similar to the raised ranch, its entry is on grade or just a few steps above, while the raised-ranch entry always is above grade. The main-level floor is a half flight of stairs up from the entry, and the lower-level area is a half flight

FIGURE 5.4 House Types

ONE-STORY HOUSE

1ST FLOOR

BASEMENT

EXPANSION ATTIC

1ST FLOOR

BASEMENT

ONE-AND-A-HALF-STORY HOUSE

down. Typically, the lower level is raised halfway out of the ground to admit natural light into the space and make the lower level more livable.

Split-Level

This generic term applies to any house that has floors located halfway between other floors. Usually, one of the floors is partially below ground level and short flights of stairs connect all levels.

Two-Story

Here, two stories are completely above ground; the entry is only a few steps above ground level. The two-story house offers the most

FIGURE 5.4   House Types (Continued)

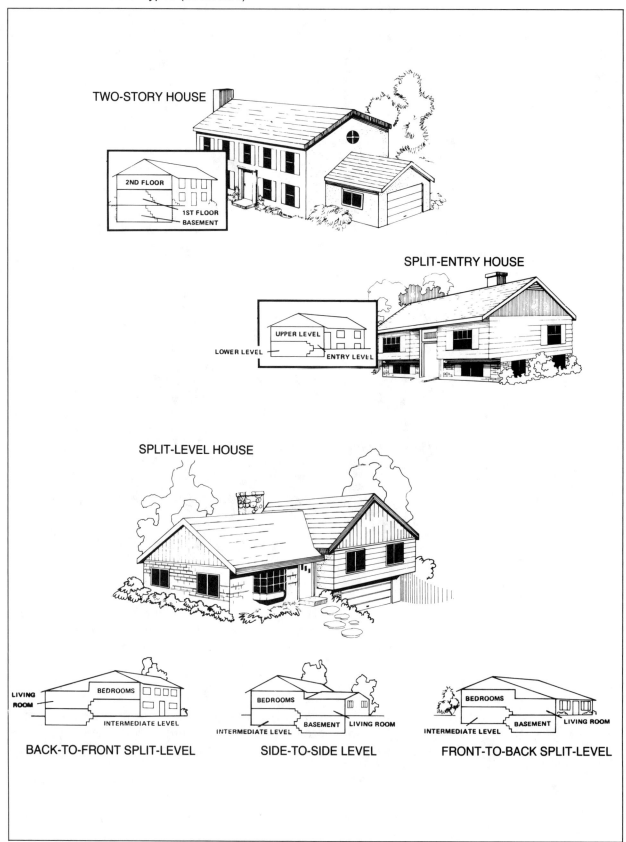

TWO-STORY HOUSE

2ND FLOOR

1ST FLOOR
BASEMENT

SPLIT-ENTRY HOUSE

UPPER LEVEL

LOWER LEVEL   ENTRY LEVEL

SPLIT-LEVEL HOUSE

LIVING
ROOM   BEDROOMS

INTERMEDIATE LEVEL

BACK-TO-FRONT SPLIT-LEVEL

BEDROOMS

INTERMEDIATE LEVEL   BASEMENT   LIVING ROOM

SIDE-TO-SIDE LEVEL

BEDROOMS

INTERMEDIATE LEVEL   BASEMENT   LIVING ROOM

FRONT-TO-BACK SPLIT-LEVEL

living space within an established perimeter; the living area is doubled on the same foundation.

Story-and-a-Half

This type is lower in profile than the two-story because the roof begins at the one-story level. The steeply pitched roof peaks high enough to allow headroom in about half of the second floor. This type also is called Cape Cod, although the term also refers to a house style.

INTERIOR DESIGN

The interior design or layout of a house is basic not only to day-to-day comfort and livability, but it affects the home's market value as well.

Two basic approaches to space must be taken into account when designing a floor plan—open and casual or separate and formal. In an open plan, fewer walls and use of half-walls create an airy atmosphere that makes spaces seem larger. Activities can overlap from room to room. On the negative side, energy costs usually are increased, and often some privacy is lost. Fewer interior walls also can mean limited spots for furniture placement.

In a less-open plan, areas can be closed off to control sound or to direct heating and cooling. If more private areas are desired, natural light should be included on as many sides as possible to avoid a closed-in look. Spaces should flow well and not appear chopped up.

Floor Plan

Living with a floor plan that doesn't feel right or doesn't conform to a family's life-style is like wearing a shoe that doesn't fit. The family never will get used to it, and they will always wish they had something else. So before a prospective buyer decides on a floor plan, he or she should take a good look at the layout and imagine how it will feel living in the spaces.

A good floor plan directs traffic smoothly and usually divides neatly into three basic areas or zones: *working* or high-activity areas, *living* or moderate-activity areas and *sleeping* or low-activity areas. The **working** zone includes the kitchen, laundry area and perhaps a workshop. The **living** zone consists of the living, dining and family rooms. The **sleeping** zone contains the bedroom. Each zone should be separated from the others so that activities in one area do not interfere with those in another. Ideally, the areas that generate the most noise should be grouped together, well away from the bedrooms.

Circulation Areas. Circulation areas, consisting of halls, stairways and entries, often make the difference between a good floor plan and a poor one.

The main entry to the house should be easily accessible to visitors. Guests should have only a short walk from the driveway to the front door. Also, the view from the entry that will greet visitors must be considered. Can the kitchen be seen when visitors come through the door? A refrigerator, for instance, shouldn't be the first thing to catch the eye. Entries, remember, are where a good many first impressions take shape.

Another important consideration in any plan is the garage-to-kitchen connection. Is there a short and convenient route for unloading groceries or taking out garbage?

A study of a floor plan will reveal traffic patterns. Can people get directly from one room to another without crossing other rooms? Is there direct access to a bathroom from any room? Is the stairway between levels located off a hallway or foyer rather than off a room?

Other Principles of Good Design. A kitchen contains three main activity areas or centers:

1. *Food storage*—includes the refrigerator/freezer, cabinets and counter space;
2. *Cooking*—includes the range, oven, counter space on either side, and cabinets and drawers for pots, pans and utensils; and
3. *Cleanup*—includes the sink, counter space on either side, a garbage disposal, a dishwasher and a trash compactor.

The efficient arrangement of these three centers is called a **work triangle** (see Figure 5.5). For maximum efficiency, the

FIGURE 5.5   Kitchen Work Triangle

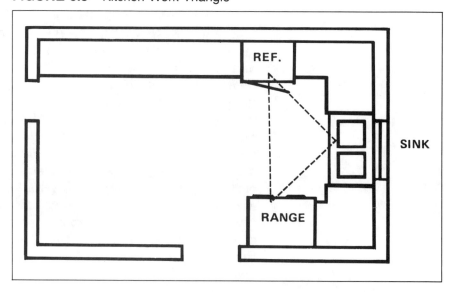

triangle should have a total perimeter of at least 12 feet but no more than 22 feet.

To save steps and time, short direct routes should connect the kitchen with all eating areas. If traffic goes through the kitchen, it should pass outside the work triangle so people won't bump into each other when someone is carrying a hot dish.

For cooks who like to keep in touch with the family while preparing meals, a kitchen that's open to the family room should be considered. This arrangement makes the space seem larger and provides a place for quick countertop meals.

If a family enjoys entertaining, or appreciates dining variety, the floor plan must cater to an assortment of dining options, whether they include an informal eating area, breakfast bar or formal dining room. All these areas must be contiguous to a food-preparation and serving location. If the family is fond of barbecuing in the backyard, a plan with an outdoor deck or patio adjacent to the kitchen is ideal.

Whatever layout is chosen for the dining and living areas, plenty of space should be available for furnishings and activities. If entertaining in small groups is desired, a family room that's cozier and more specialized than a formal living room would be preferred. A formal living room, however, offers the flexibility of an intimate conversation or reading area.

Privacy is the key to any successful bedroom arrangement. Sleeping areas should be secluded from living and working areas, especially for families with children or for those who entertain frequently.

In the master bath, locating the vanity in a separate area from the toilet, tub and shower makes it easier for a couple to get ready for the day and also will keep the mirror from steaming up from the hot water in the tub and shower. If a person enjoys relaxing after a stressful day by taking a hot bath, lifting weights or doing aerobics, the possibility of including a convenient exercise area, sauna or whirlpool tub should be considered.

A full bath near the secondary bedrooms adds to the convenience and privacy of other family members and overnight guests. A half-bath near the kitchen and living areas will keep guests from invading the home's private spaces.

Laundry facilities should be placed close to bedrooms and bathrooms. Proximity to the kitchen makes it convenient to wash and dry while cooking or cleaning there.

Figure 5.6 lists the main flaws to watch for when evaluating a floor plan.

Throughout the rest of this chapter many construction terms and concepts will be presented and discussed. As needed, refer to the Anatomy of a House diagram in Appendix C. The diagram identifies the different parts of a house and shows how they fit together as a whole.

FIGURE 5.6   Floor Plan Checklist

	YES	NO
1. Are main interior zones—living, working, sleeping—clearly separated?	____	____
2. Does the front door enter into a foyer—not directly into the living room?	____	____
3. Is there a front hall closet?	____	____
4. Is there direct access from the front door to the kitchen, bathroom and bedrooms without passing through other rooms?	____	____
5. Is the rear door convenient to the kitchen and easy to reach from the street, driveway and garage?	____	____
6. Is there a comfortable eating space for the family in or near the kitchen?	____	____
7. Is a separate dining area or dining room convenient to the kitchen?	____	____
8. Is a stairway located in a hallway or foyer instead of between levels of a room?	____	____
9. Are bedrooms concealed from the living room or foyer?	____	____
10. Are walls between bedrooms soundproof? (They should be separated by a bathroom or closet.)	____	____
11. Is the recreation room or family room well located?	____	____
12. Is the basement accessible from outside?	____	____
13. Are outdoor living areas accessible from the kitchen?	____	____
14. Are walls uninterrupted by doors and windows that could complicate furniture arrangement?	____	____
15. Does the kitchen have enough storage space? Counter space? Lighting?	____	____
16. Is the work triangle efficient?	____	____
17. Are kitchen work areas separate from heavy traffic areas?	____	____
18. Is the kitchen modern enough?	____	____
19. Does the house have a full bathroom on each floor?	____	____
20. Is there adequate closet space throughout the house?	____	____
21. Is the laundry area in a satisfactory location?	____	____
22. Is the garage wide and long enough?	____	____
23. Does the garage have direct access to the kitchen?	____	____

FOUNDATION

A foundation supports the weight of the house and its contents (see Figure 5.7). It is the substructure on which the superstructure rests. The foundation includes the footings, foundation walls, pilasters, slab and all other parts that provide support for the house and distribute the weight of the superstructure to the underlying earth.

Poured concrete is by far the best of all foundation materials. Because of its strength and resistance to moisture, it is particularly good for keeping basements dry. Other foundations may be constructed of cut stone, stone and brick and concrete block.

Exterior Foundation Inspection

Walk around the perimeter of the house and inspect the foundation. The foundation should be exposed for six to eight inches above ground. Pay particular attention to any areas that appear

FIGURE 5.7   Foundation

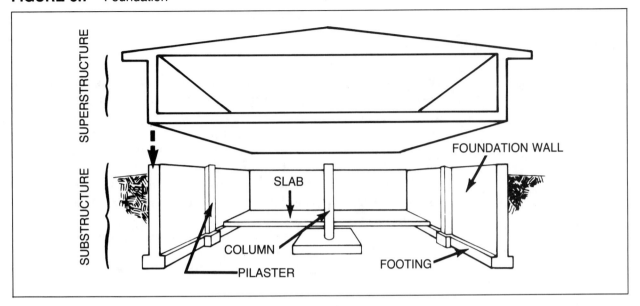

to be settling. Settlement is caused by the compression of soil under the foundation. All houses settle. The uneven settlement of the foundation, especially at the corners, however, is a sure sign of trouble. Uneven settlement is evidenced also by cracks in foundation walls, cracks in finished walls and ceilings, floors that slope and windows and doors that fit poorly.

Check for cracks and signs of water penetration. Peeling paint on a concrete foundation may indicate moisture buildup in the basement. Soil should be graded away from the foundation to allow runoff water to flow away from the house. Look for signs of runoff pooling against the foundation. Check to see that downspouts have splash plates to channel water away.

Basement

A basement is the lowest level of a house and usually is left unfinished by the builder. The exterior walls of a basement also are the foundation walls of the house. Exposed foundation walls can tell you a lot about the structural soundness of the house. For example, curves or bows in the foundation walls may indicate excessive weight being applied to that area.

Does the basement smell musty or feel damp? Look for signs of water penetration—discoloration along the lower wall surfaces; white powdery deposits called **efflorescence** on exposed concrete (mineral salts in masonry that dissolve in water and pass through to the surface); damp wood sills (these rest on the foundation and support the wall framing); or discoloration of framing members.

Check the location of any foundation cracks identified on your external examination. Does water appear to have entered through them? A leaky basement is one of the biggest headaches a homeowner can have and often is difficult and expensive to correct.

Termite Damage and Wood Rot

Before concrete for the foundation is poured, the ground should be chemically treated to poison termites—antlike insects that are very destructive to wood. This will prevent them from coming up through or around the foundation and into the wooden structure. The chemical treatment of the lumber used for sills and beams and the installation of metal termite shields also will provide protection.

When checking for termites, look for fuzzy white columns of tubes snaking up the foundation. Termites and wood rot can destroy wood from inside, with little visible evidence. Examine any wood adjacent to the foundation, such as siding or porch supports. If you question its soundness, probe it with a screwdriver. If the wood feels like cork, it has been eaten away inside.

Carpenter Ants and Powder-Post Beetles

Carpenter ants and powder-post beetles are other insects that cause damage to wood. Damage by carpenter ants can be recognized by the presence of hollow, irregular, clean chambers cut across the grain of partially decayed wood. The most obvious sign of powder-post beetles are small round holes in the infested wood. The beetles exit through these holes after they have done their work.

Radon Gas

Radon is a colorless, odorless, tasteless radioactive gas found in most rocks and soils. Outdoors, it mixes with the air and is found in low concentrations that are harmless to people. Indoors, however, it can accumulate and build up to dangerous levels that can increase the risk of lung cancer.

Besides the most immediate concern about radon—the threat of cancer—homeowners also are worried about the impact of high radon levels on the value of real estate. According to legal experts, sellers may be held responsible retroactively for corrective measures if testing shows that a house was sold with dangerously high levels of radon gas. This is in keeping with recent developments in disclosure and negligence law. In some states, sellers must give written notice of any problems affecting the value of the property being sold. Failure to find and disclose the presence of dangerous radon levels to a buyer could be held by a court of law to constitute negligence. The problem is that radon gas levels may vary from day to day and even week to week. They are affected by barometric pressure, rainfall, wind and temperature.

Figure 5.8 shows how radon gas can enter a home.

FIGURE 5.8 Common Radon Entry Routes

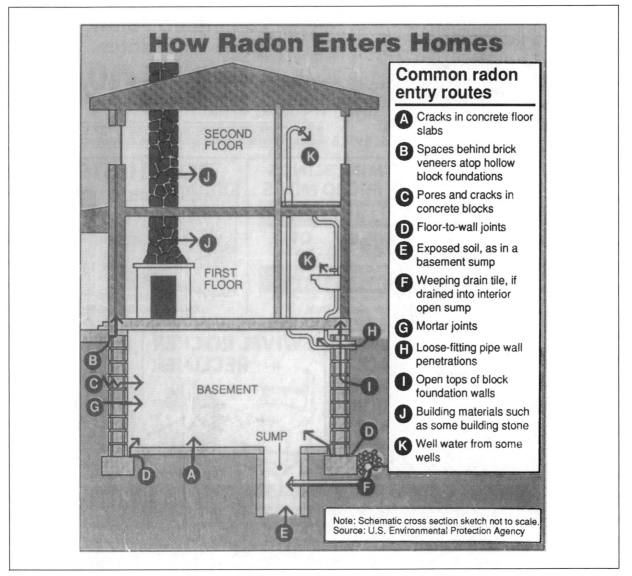

FRAMING

After the foundation is in place, the house is ready for **framing.** A house's frame or skeleton gives shape and strength to the building. It usually is made of pieces of lumber nailed together to create a framework of floors, walls and roof. The frame then is covered with sheets of insulating material or plywood.

After the skeleton of the house is constructed, **sheathing** is nailed directly to the wall studs to form the base for siding. Plywood panels used to be the most popular sheathing material for walls. They are the strongest and most rigid option, but they are expensive and don't insulate well. Now they sometimes are used on corners to lend stability, paired with better

FIGURE 5.9   Roof Designs

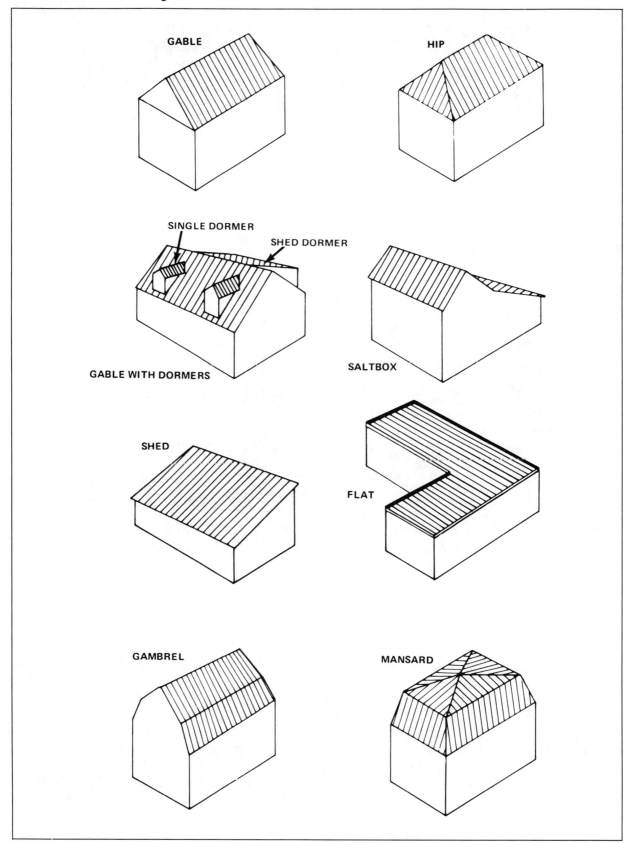

FIGURE 5.10   Eave or Cornice

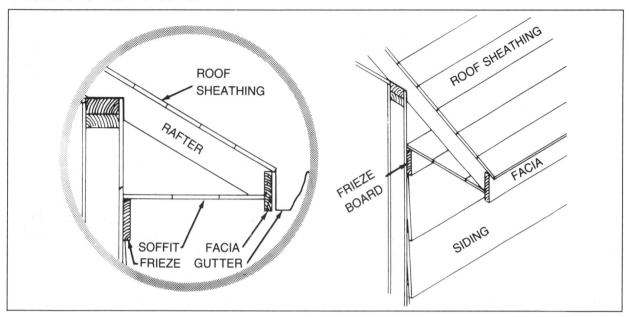

insulators such as fiberboard combinations and polyurethane foam panels.

The roof on a house does more to set it apart from other houses than any other single architectural feature. Some of the most commonly used roof styles or designs are shown in Figure 5.9.

EXTERIOR TRIM

The overhang of a pitched roof that extends beyond the exterior walls of a house is called an **eave,** or **cornice,** shown in Figure 5.10. The cornice is composed of the soffit, the frieze board, the facia board and the extended rafters. The **frieze board** is the exterior wood-trim board used to finish the exterior wall between the top of the siding or masonry and the eave, or overhang, of the roof framing. The **facia board** is an exterior wood trim used along the line of the butt end of the rafters where the roof overhangs the structural walls. The overhang of the cornice provides a decorative touch to the exterior of a house as well as some protection from the sun and rain.

ROOF COVERINGS

The roof is a key design element as well as a barrier against rain and snow. It is composed of a moisture-resistant felt underlayment or base, topped with a surface material.

Asphalt Shingles

Most houses are roofed with asphalt shingles. They come in 12- by 36-inch strips that, when overlapped and nailed in place, give the appearance of individual shingles.

Two basic types of asphalt shingles are available. One type is **organic,** made by impregnating a mat of cellulose fibers with asphalt and surfacing it with ceramic-coated mineral granules. A newer type, **inorganic,** is made the same way but with a base mat of fiberglass. Fiberglass shingles are lighter, stronger and last longer than comparable organic shingles.

Wood Shingles and Shakes

If a house doesn't have an asphalt shingle roof, it probably is covered with wood shingles or shakes. Shingles and shakes usually are made from cedar, which naturally resists decay. They can be treated to maintain their natural color or left to weather to a silvery gray or light tan, depending on climatic conditions. Flammability is a drawback. Wood shingles and shakes can be treated with fire-resistant chemicals, but the process is expensive. Wood shingles and shakes are more expensive than asphalt shingles.

Clay or Concrete Tiles

Clay tiles are made in flat shingles, S shapes and barrel shapes. They're most popular teamed with stucco exteriors to achieve a Spanish look. Clay tiles are durable enough to last a home's lifetime, but they require a stronger roof structure to support the additional weight.

Concrete tiles can resemble clay tiles, slate or shakes. They're gaining in popularity because they're durable, relatively inexpensive, lighter and easier to install than clay tiles. In fact, some varieties are light enough to be installed on a standard roof; that is, the roof framing would not have to be reinforced to withstand the weight.

Slate

Slate shingles are among the most expensive roofing materials available, but they can last a home's lifetime and add to its market value. Like clay tiles, slate is quite heavy and may require extra strong framing for a house.

Metal

Metal roofs usually are aluminum. Other options include stainless steel, copper and galvanized steel. Corrugated panels, flat sheets, shingles and shake look-alikes are among the products offered. Aluminum roofs can last as long as 35 years; copper can last longer. Cost can be moderate to expensive, depending on the type of metal selected. For example, copper would cost much more than galvanized steel.

Because of qualities such as strength, light weight, durability and ease of installation, metals, according to most experts, will capture more of the residential roofing market in coming years. On the negative side, metal roofing material is susceptible to corrosion and it expands and contracts as the temperature changes.

Roll Roofing

Roll roofing is similar to asphalt shingles, but comes in wide strips that are lapped horizontally. It is less expensive than many other forms of roofing and generally is used on shallow slopes because it has fewer places that would allow standing water to leak. Roll roofing generally won't last as long as shingles, however, and it's more prone to cracks, tears and blisters.

EXTERIOR SIDING

Siding constitutes much of the decorative element of a home's exterior and is one of the main things a potential buyer will notice. It must look good and stand up to climatic conditions, too.

Exterior siding should be appropriate to the style of the house and should harmonize with its surroundings—the landscape and other homes in the neighborhood.

Solid Wood Siding

Cedar is a commonly used, high-quality siding. Redwood lap siding is another durable choice, although it's more expensive. Other options include pine and spruce, which are less costly.

Well-cared-for, solid lumber can last the lifetime of a home. A vapor barrier beneath the wood will prevent condensation from moisture inside the house that can rot wood and cause paint to peel.

Wood Shingles and Shakes

Wood shingles and shakes, made of cedar, cypress or redwood, are naturally resistant to moisture and insect infestation. They don't require painting or staining except to change colors. Shingles and shakes are moderate to expensive in cost, depending on the grade of the wood.

Plywood Siding

Plywood siding is made of thin sheets of wood bonded together with waterproof adhesive. The outer veneer is available in about 75 wood species. Because plywood siding comes in large panels, installation is fast, and with fewer joints, air infiltration and noise are reduced.

Hardboard Siding

Hardboard is manufactured from wood fibers compressed into sheets. Hardboard surfaces range from smooth to textured and sometimes replicate wood grains. Hardboard siding is extremely durable and highly resistant to denting and gouging.

Aluminum Siding

Aluminum siding has long been used to resurface older houses but now is a strong competitor with wood and other materials on the exterior of new houses in all price classes. It is available with a baked-enamel or vinyl finish and is fireproof and virtually maintenance-free.

Aluminum siding should be backed with fiberboard or polystyrene foam to improve its insulating characteristics, to make it more dent-resistant and to reduce the noise created by wind, rain and hail.

Vinyl Siding

Vinyl siding is applied in much the same way as aluminum siding and is similar in appearance. Vinyl doesn't dent like aluminum does, however, and the color runs throughout the product, so chips and scratches are not easy to see. Because vinyl expands and contracts with temperature changes more than other materials, proper installation is important to avoid buckling or rippling.

Stucco

Stucco is a type of mortar that lends itself to Spanish-inspired architecture. It is noted for its durability, insulation and resistance to fire, insects and mildew.

Brick and Stone Veneers

Brick and stone veneers are expensive but can increase the market value of a home. They are popular because they are attractive and fire-resistant and require little maintenance. Stonework generally is more costly than brickwork. Figure 5.11 shows a cutaway of a brick-veneered exterior wall, the most common type of masonry material used on houses.

Solid brick and stone are seldom used today as structural walls because of the expense involved. They require extra-thick foundation walls, and craftspeople able to install them are scarce.

INSULATION

Properly insulating a home can reduce costly energy loss—helping the homeowner save on fuel bills during both the heating and cooling seasons. Fiberglass and rock wool are commonly used insulation materials.

Figure 5.12 shows the four areas where home insulation is required.

FIGURE 5.11   Cutaway of Brick-Veneered Wall

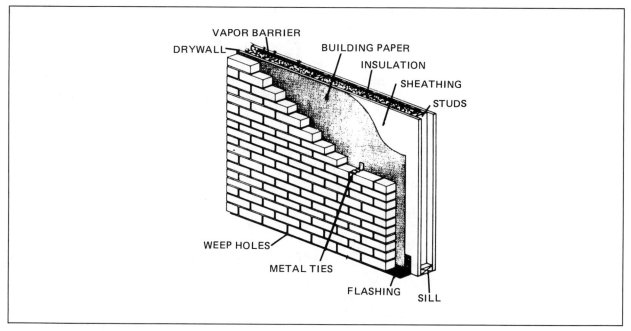

FIGURE 5.12   Areas That Require Insulation

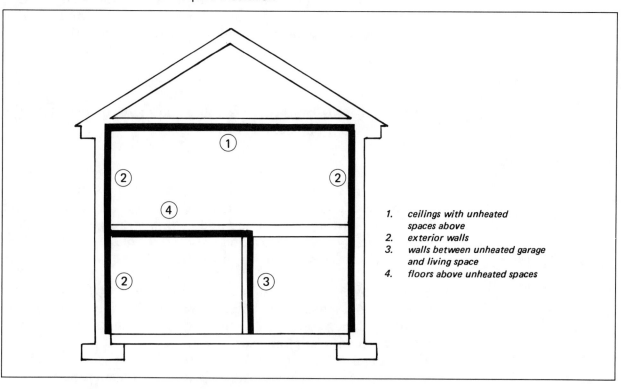

1. ceilings with unheated spaces above
2. exterior walls
3. walls between unheated garage and living space
4. floors above unheated spaces

Insulation performance is rated in terms of **R-values. R** means resistance to heat flow. The higher the R-value, the greater the insulating power.

How much R-value is needed? The U.S. Department of Energy (DOE) recently has upgraded its insulation recommendations to homeowners, increasing its suggested minimum R-value to accommodate the country's various climates. The new R-values now are specific to zip-code areas and take into account climate, heating and cooling needs, types of heating used and energy prices. The new guidelines cover insulation requirements for ceilings, floors, exterior walls, attics and crawl spaces. Check with local authorities for the insulating needs in your area.

Asbestos and Urea Formaldehyde

Two kinds of home insulation to avoid using are asbestos and urea formaldehyde. Asbestos insulation, installed in ceilings and walls of older homes, no longer is used because it is believed to cause cancer if its fibers get into the lungs. Urea formaldehyde also may be a potential health hazard, and its use is banned in most parts of the United States. It often emits noxious odors and toxic fumes, causing nausea and other irritations if inhaled. If you suspect a house has either asbestos or urea-formaldehyde insulation, consult a qualified inspector to examine all questionable areas.

EXTERIOR WINDOWS AND DOORS

Windows and doors contribute to the design and appearance of a house as well as provide a specific function. Skillfully placed doors regulate traffic patterns through the house and provide protection from intruders. Windows, in turn, admit light and a view of the outside.

Types of Windows

Figure 5.13 illustrates and describes the most common types of windows found in homes.

Energy-Efficient Windows

Energy-efficient windows consist of frames made of good insulating material that enclose insulating glass. In addition, proper installation, weather stripping and caulking are crucial. For example, a 1/16-inch crack around a 3×5-foot window is equivalent to having a brick-size hole in the wall.

Frames. Vinyl- and metal-clad wood frames are best for energy efficiency and low maintenance. Other frame options include solid wood, solid vinyl and metal, usually aluminum. Wood frames, although good insulators, need paint and upkeep and can rot or warp (unless clad in vinyl or aluminum). Aluminum and vinyl windows, although good for upkeep, are poor insulators.

FIGURE 5.13   Common Window Types

Double-Hung

The double-hung window has both an upper and lower sash that slides vertically along separate tracks. This arrangement allows cool air to come in at the bottom and warm air to go out through the top.

Horizontal Sliding

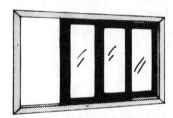

The horizontal sliding window moves back and forth on tracks. As with the double-hung type, only 50 percent of this window can be opened for fresh air.

Casement

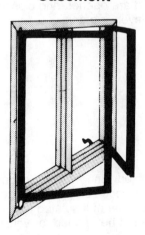

Casement windows are hinged at the side and open outward. One advantage of the casement window is that the entire window can be opened for ventilation.

FIGURE 5.13   Common Window Types (Continued)

Awning

An awning window is hinged at the top and swings open at the bottom, providing good ventilation and protection from the rain.

Hopper

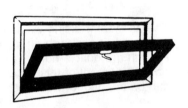

A hopper window is hinged at the bottom and opens into the room. It is best suited to a basement, where the hopper opens above head level and there is little danger of bumping into it.

Jalousie

Jalousie, or louver, windows consist of a series of overlapping horizontal glass louvers that pivot together in a common frame and are opened and closed with a lever or crank.

Fixed

A fixed window usually consists of a wood sash with a large single pane of insulated glass that cannot be opened for ventilation.

SOURCE: William L. Ventolo, Jr., *The Complete Home Inspection Kit* (Chicago: Dearborn Financial Publishing, Inc., 1990), 67.

Glass. **Low-E** glass refers to a low-emissivity film coating on double-glazed windows. Double-glazed means a window has two panes of glass with a sealed air space between them. The invisible film blocks ultraviolet rays from the sun that cause fabrics to fade and at the same time, boosts insulation. If the air space is filled with argon gas, windows with Low-E coatings offer even more insulation value.

Noise Pollution. Windows can leak sound, just as pipes can leak water. Factors ranging from window design and materials to installation techniques affect the noise levels in homes. In general, though, energy-efficient windows cut down on the amount of sound entering a home.

Air absorbs sound and glass carries it. As a result, double- or triple-pane windows absorb more sound waves than do single-pane windows. Wood and vinyl frames absorb more sound than aluminum frames. In addition, applying soft materials such as foam or caulking around the frame will increase sound absorption even more.

Location of Exterior Doors

Exterior doors control passage in and out of the house. The **main entrance** door, usually the most attractive and most prominent door, should be located on the street side of the house. The goal is to create a good first impression and make the entry easy to find. The **service** door leads outside from rooms such as the kitchen, utility room, basement or garage and is important for good traffic flow in the house. The **patio** door ties together indoors and outdoors and usually opens from a family room or dining area onto a patio, porch or terrace.

Types of Doors

Doors are most often classified by construction and appearance—the four most common types are flush, panel, sliding glass and storm and screen (see Figure 5.14).

Wood doors are available in solid wood (plank), veneer over solid wood or veneer over a hollow core. Solid cores generally are preferred for exterior doors because they have better insulation qualities and are more resistant to warping. Hollow-core doors are lighter than the solid-core type and are used for interior locations, where heat and sound insulation are not so critical.

Steel and aluminum doors are not solid metal but have a lighter inner core of wood, wood and foam or rigid foam. The aluminum or steel exterior surface comes primed or with a baked-enamel finish and doesn't swell or shrink. It's also weather-resistant and fire-retardant.

Sliding glass doors contain one or more panels that slide in a frame of metal or wood. The panels may hold either single-pane

FIGURE 5.14 Types of Doors

PANEL

FLUSH

SCREEN DOOR

SLIDING GLASS

or insulating glass depending on the local climate. Some glass doors provide self-storing screens in a separate track of the door frame.

Storm doors are made either with fixed glass panels, to improve weather resistance, or with both screen and glass inserts, to permit ventilation and insect control. In areas with moderate year-round temperatures, screen doors (without glass inserts) frequently are used. Combination doors combine the functions of both storm and screen doors with interchangeable glass and screen panels. Self-storing storm doors contain the equivalent of a two-track window, accommodating two inserts in one track and another in the adjacent track. The glass and screen inserts slide up and down just as they do in a vertical storm window.

INTERIOR WALLS AND FINISHING

Interior walls are the partitioning dividers for individual rooms and usually are covered with **wallboard,** although lath and plaster sometimes is used. The terms *drywall* and *plasterboard* are synonymous with wallboard. Wallboard is finished by a process known as *taping* and *floating*. **Taping** covers the joints between the sheets of wallboard. **Floating** is the process of smoothing out the walls by applying a plaster texture over the joints and rough edges where nails attach the wallboard to the wall studs. Texturing may be used in some areas as a final coating applied with a roller onto the wallboard prior to painting.

The final features added to a home include *floor covering, trim, cabinetwork* and *wall finishings* of paint, wallpaper or paneling.

Floor coverings of vinyl, wood (either in strips or blocks), carpet, brick, stone or terrazzo tile are applied over the wood or concrete subflooring.

Trim masks the joints between the walls and ceiling and gives a finished decorator touch to the room. Trim, which is made of wood, hardboard or vinyl, should be selected in a style that is complementary to the overall decor of the house.

Cabinetwork may be either built in on the job or prefabricated in the mill. Cabinets should be well constructed to open and close properly and should conform to the style of the house.

Wall finishing is one of the most important decorator items in the home. Paint and wallpaper should be selected for both beauty and utility. Prefinished wood fiber and plastic panels such as polyethylene-covered plywood paneling now are widely used in less formal rooms. Either ceramic or plastic tiles still are used extensively as bathroom wall coverings.

PLUMBING

The plumbing system in a house is actually a number of separate systems, each designed to serve a special function. The **water-supply** system brings water to the house from the city main or from a well and distributes hot and cold water through two sets of pipes. The **drainage system** collects waste and used water from fixtures and carries it away to a central point for disposal outside the house. The **vent-piping system** carries out of the house all sewer gases that develop in drainage lines. It also equalizes air pressure within the waste system so that waste will flow away and not back up into the fixtures. The **waste-collecting system** is needed only when the main waste drain in the house is lower than the sewer level under the street or when the house has more than one drainage system. The **house connection-pipe system,** a single pipe, is the waste connection from the house to the city sewer line, to a septic tank or to some other waste-disposal facility.

Plumbing must be installed subject to strict inspections and in accordance with local building codes, which dictate the materials to be used and the method of installation. Sewer pipes are made of cast iron, concrete or plastic, while water pipes are made of copper, plastic or galvanized iron. Recently, wrought-drawn copper and plastic have been used more frequently because they eliminate the need for piping joints in the foundation slab.

Plumbing Fixtures

Bathtubs, toilets and sinks are made of cast iron or pressed steel coated with enamel. Fiberglass is a newer material for these fixtures and is gaining in popularity. Plumbing fixtures have relatively long lives and often are replaced because of their obsolete style long before they have worn out.

Water Heaters

A water heater is basically an insulated metal tank that does just what its name implies. The size needed will depend on several factors including the number of people in the family, the hot-water consumption during peak use periods (such as bathing or laundering), the recovery time required by the tank and fuel costs in the area. Manufacturers recommend that the tank be placed closest to the point of use.

Water is almost always heated by gas or electricity. Water heaters are available in several capacities for residential use, ranging from 17 gallons up to 80 gallons. Although a 30-gallon water heater is usually the minimum size installed, most families require a 40- to 50-gallon tank. After water is heated to a predetermined temperature, the heater automatically shuts off. When hot water is drained off, cold water replaces it, and the heating unit turns on automatically.

HEATING AND AIR-CONDITIONING

Warm-air heating systems are most prevalent in today's houses. A forced warm-air system consists of a furnace, warm-air distributing ducts and ducts for the return of cool air. All supply ducts should be well insulated and joints and other openings taped to prevent air leaks.

Each furnace has a capacity rated in British Thermal Units (BTUs). The number of BTUs given represents the furnace's heat output from either gas, oil or electric firing. A heating and cooling engineer can determine the cubic area of the house, as well as its construction, insulation and window and door sizes, and from this data, compute the furnace capacity required to provide heat for the house in the coldest possible weather.

All gas pipes for heating and cooking are made of black iron. Gas pipes are installed in the walls or run overhead in the attic, where adequate ventilation is possible. They are never placed in the slab.

Almost all new homes today are centrally air conditioned. Air-conditioning units are rated either in BTUs or in tons. Twelve thousand BTUs are the equivalent of a one-ton capacity. An engineer can determine the measurements and problems inherent in the construction and layout of the space and from this information can specify the cooling capacity required to service the space or house adequately.

Combination heating and cooling systems are common in new homes. The most prevalent is the conventional warm-air heating system with a cooling unit attached. The same ducts and blower that force warm air are used to force cool air. The cooling unit is similar to a large air conditioner.

Many heating experts believe the heat pump eventually will replace today's conventional combination heating and cooling systems. The small heat pump is a single piece of equipment that uses the same components for heating or cooling. The most commonly used system for small heat pumps takes heat out of the ground or air in winter to warm the air in the house and takes warm air out of the house in summer, replacing it with cooler air. The main drawback to the heat pump has been its initial cost. Once installed, however, it operates very economically and requires little maintenance. It works most efficiently in climates where winter weather is not severe, but new improvements make it adequate even in northern states.

Technical aspects of heating and air-conditioning should be handled by an experienced and qualified authority, although the homeowner should give due consideration to the operation and maintenance of the unit. Filters should be cleaned regularly and return air grilles and registers should be clear and clean for passage of the circulating air. The thermostat controls should be completely understood and properly set. The compressor and fan motors should be cared for on a regular maintenance schedule.

Solar Heating

The increased demand for fossil fuels in recent years has forced builders to look for new sources of energy. One of the most promising sources of heat for residential buildings is **solar energy.** The two methods for gathering solar energy are *passive* and *active.* The simplest form of solar heating is a **passive** system in which windows on the south side of a house take advantage of winter sunlight. A passive system can be improved inside the house by using water-filled containers, which are warmed by the sun during the day, to reradiate warmth into the room during the night. Such a system takes up space inside the home, however, and is not compatible with most decorating schemes. If these considerations are unimportant, and if there is adequate available sunlight, a passive solar heating system can be installed easily and at low cost.

Most solar heating units suitable for residential use are **active** systems that operate by gathering the heat from the sun's rays with one or more **solar collectors** (see Figure 5.15). Water or air is forced through a series of pipes in the solar collector to be heated by the sun's rays. The hot air or water then is stored in a heavily insulated storage tank until it is needed to heat the house.

On a related note, solar heaters for swimming pools continue to provide a low-cost way of heating pool water. Solar pool heaters, in fact, constitute the largest single use for solar equipment.

The U.S. government is one of the best sources on solar topics—whether for general information, the names of companies or

FIGURE 5.15   Active Solar Water-Heating System

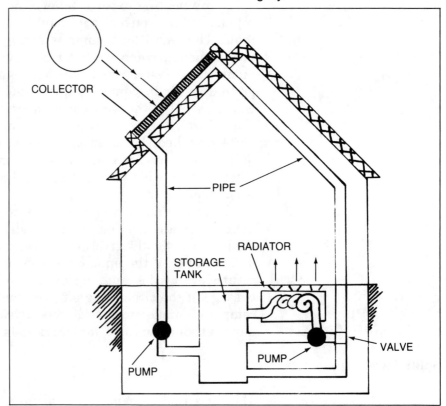

organizations in the business, the names of architects familiar with solar design or suggested references for further study.

ELECTRICAL SYSTEM

A good residential electrical system must have three important characteristics. First, it must meet all National Electrical Code (NEC) safety requirements: Each major appliance should have its own circuit, and lighting circuits should be isolated from electrical equipment that causes fluctuations in voltage. Second, the system must meet the home's existing needs and must have the capacity to accommodate room additions and new appliances. Finally, it should be convenient; there should be enough switches, lights and outlets located so that occupants will not have to walk in the dark or use extension cords.

Electrical service from the power company is brought into the home through the transformer and the meter into a **circuit breaker box** (or a **fused panel** in older homes). The circuit breaker box is the distribution panel for the many electrical circuits in the house. In case of a power overload, the heat generated by the additional flow of electrical power will cause the circuit breaker to open at the breaker box, thus reducing the possibility of electrical fires. The architect or the builder is responsible for adhering to local building codes, which regulate electrical wiring. All electrical installations are inspected by the local building authorities, which assures the homeowner of the system's compliance with the building codes.

Residential wiring circuits are rated by the voltage that they are designed to carry. In the past, most residences were wired only for 110-volt capacity. Today, because of the many built-in appliances in use, 220-volt to 240-volt service is generally necessary. **Amperage,** the strength of a current expressed in amperes, is shown on the circuit breaker panel. The circuit breaker panel (or fuse panel) should have a capacity of at least 100 amperes. A larger service (150 to 200 or more amperes) may be needed if there is electric heat or an electric range or if the house has more than 3,000 square feet. New wiring will be required if the existing board's capacity is only 30 to 60 amperes. If there are fewer than eight or ten circuits, it probably will be necessary to add more. Each circuit is represented by a separate circuit breaker or fuse. A house with a lot of electrical equipment may require 15 to 20 or more circuits.

The construction checklist in the Appraisal Worksheet is a guideline to help you inspect the construction features and concepts that were covered in this chapter.

APPRAISAL WORKSHEET

External Inspection

_____ 1. *Grading:* Be sure the ground around the foundation slopes away from the house. Look for signs of erosion or standing water in the yard.

_____ 2. *Foundation:* Make sure there are no serious cracks in the foundation or signs of uneven settling. Be sure the foundation's drainage system will direct water away from the house. Check that a nondeteriorating vapor barrier has been installed below the slab so that moisture will not creep through into the finished structure.

_____ 3. *Roof:* Shingles should be flat and secure. Check to see that flashing is in place around the chimney and where roof edges meet walls. Gutters and downspouts should be held securely in place. Splash blocks should carry water away from the house. Check the eaves for signs of rot or decay.

_____ 4. *Siding:* Note the type (wood, stucco, masonry, aluminum, vinyl) and condition of the siding. Check wood siding for bubbled or flaking paint, which may mean that the house has insufficient vapor-barrier protection. Probe wood siding for rot, especially the bottom boards along the foundation. Note bulges or cracks in stucco; deteriorating mortar between bricks or stones as well as breakdown of the bricks; and dents, chips or cracks in aluminum or vinyl siding.

Check the trim around the doors and windows and at the corners of the house. It should be firmly in place and well caulked. There should be a tight seal where siding meets chimney masonry.

Interior Inspection

_____ 1. *Basement and attic:* Check for any indication of dampness or leaks in the basement. Look for cracks in foundation walls and in basement floors. Look over all exposed components (floor joists, support columns, insulation, electrical wiring, heating ducts and plumbing) for obvious defects and improper workmanship.

Check inside the attic for leaks. Carefully look over each rafter. Use a screwdriver to poke any suspicious-looking spots for possible wood rot.

_____ 2. *Doors and windows:* Open and shut all windows and doors to make sure they operate properly and seal tightly. Check for broken or cracked glass in windows. Make sure there are no holes in the screens. Check that both windows and doors are weather-stripped.

_____ 3. *Floors:* Walk across all floors to check for squeaks. Carpet should be in reasonably good shape and should be tightly stretched with nearly invisible seams. Check for ridges or seam gaps in vinyl tile or sheet flooring. The finish of wood floors should be smooth and even.

_____ 4. *Finishes:* Check paint and varnish finishes in all rooms, including closets and stairways. Check the condition of wallpaper and paneling. Make sure all trim and molding is in place.

_____ 5. *Equipment:* Try all faucets and plumbing fixtures, including toilets, tubs and showers. Turn on all heating-cooling and water-heating units to make sure that they operate properly. Check the draft and the damper on fireplaces. Check equipment such as the intercom system, garage door opener and doorbell. Make sure kitchen appliances are operable.

6

The Sales
Comparison Approach

Let's review briefly the three ways to estimate real estate value:

1. With the *cost approach,* the appraiser calculates the cost of building a comparable structure on a similar site.
2. Using the *income approach,* the appraiser computes value based on the rental income the property is capable of producing.
3. Applying the *sales comparison approach,* the appraiser compares the value of the property with others similar to it that have been sold recently.

The sales comparison approach is the most widely used method of valuing residential property and is the approach that will be covered in this chapter.

BASICS OF THE SALES COMPARISON APPROACH

The sales comparison approach is an empirical investigation in which the appraiser collects, classifies, analyzes and interprets market data and predicts the most probable selling price of a property.

The basic steps in the sales comparison approach are to:

*   Identify the sources of value or characteristics of the subject property that would produce market demand. This takes into account the viewpoint of and all the considerations that might influence the typical buyer.

- Find recently sold comparable properties that are reasonable alternatives for the typical buyer.
- Compare the comparable properties to the subject property and adjust for differences.
- Reach a final conclusion of value as of the date of the appraisal.

The formula for the sales comparison approach is:

$$\text{Sales Price of Comparable Property} \overset{+}{-} \text{Adjustments} = \text{Indicated Value of Subject Property}$$

The sales comparison approach is based on the principle of substitution. That is, the value of a property tends to equal the cost of acquiring a comparable property on the open market. This is just one of the principles that helps determine the value of a property.

Data for Sales Comparison Approach

When using the sales comparison approach, data is collected on sales of comparable properties. Only recent sales should be considered—properties that have been sold within the past six months; they must have been arm's-length transactions and the properties sold must be substantially similar to the subject property.

APPRAISAL PROCESS

Figure 3.2 on page 28 shows the process the appraiser follows when carrying out an assignment. If the steps in this flowchart are followed carefully, all the necessary information will be collected to arrive at an accurate appraisal. The process begins with a definition of the problem or assignment and ends with the final estimate of value.

APPLYING THE SALES COMPARISON APPROACH

Now let's follow the progress of a typical home appraisal using the sales comparison approach.

The subject property is a seven-room, brick, ranch-type house in a middle-class neighborhood. The appraiser's job is to estimate its market value.

The key to an accurate appraisal lies in methodical data collection. Much of the general data about the nation, region and city can be found in the appraiser's own files and will take little fieldwork to gather. Let's assume that these general types of information already have been collected and that the appraiser is ready to begin the analysis at the neighborhood level. Neighborhood data is the only type of general information that will necessitate conducting significant fieldwork.

Neighborhood Data and Analysis

The value of a property often is more influenced by its surroundings than by the property itself. That's why it is important to analyze the neighborhood. Here are some other reasons:

1. The neighborhood is the immediate environment of the subject—and no property can have a value higher than that set by its neighborhood.
2. Lacking sales in the immediate neighborhood, it may be necessary to collect information on sales in reasonably comparable neighborhoods—and the appraiser needs the data on which to base comparisons.
3. Neighborhood data provides background information. This is especially important if the appraisal report is to be submitted to someone who is not familiar with the area in which the subject property is located.

The appraiser can gather neighborhood information most systematically by using a form such as the one shown in Figure 6.1. This form contains all the basic data needed to make a residential appraisal report.

Armed with the neighborhood data form and a subdivision map of the area (see Figure 6.2), the appraiser is ready for the field phase of the operation. This includes driving through the streets of the area, as well as checking background facts with banks, brokers, city hall and other sources.

Neighborhood Boundaries.   A neighborhood has a distinct identity. Several factors set a neighborhood apart from surrounding areas. Neighborhood boundaries often are established by natural barriers, such as rivers, lakes and hills, or by human-made barriers, such as streets, highways and rail lines. Boundaries also may be created by differences in land use, the income level of residents, the average value of homes, city limits, census tracts, political divisions, school districts and other factors.

Figure 6.2 shows that the subject neighborhood is bounded on the north by Osceola Avenue, which separates the single-family subject neighborhood from park-district land and multifamily residences. Damper Street is the southern boundary where land use changes from residential to commercial. Tingley Avenue is the western boundary because it separates the subject neighborhood from an area of larger, older but more expensive homes. A small lake to the east of Bayshore Drive forms a physical barrier.

Life Cycle.   A residential neighborhood is constantly undergoing changes in its life cycle. The life of a neighborhood usually involves the following stages:

1. Growth—a period during which the neighborhood is being built up.

FIGURE 6.1   Neighborhood Data Form

NEIGHBORHOOD DATA FORM

BOUNDARIES:	ADJACENT TO:
NORTH *Osceola Avenue*	*Park District land & multi family res.*
SOUTH *Damper Street*	*commercial area*
EAST *Bayshore Drive*	*small lake*
WEST *Tingley Avenue*	*expensive homes*

TOPOGRAPHY: *flat; gently slopes to street* ☐ URBAN ☒ SUBURBAN ☐ RURAL

STAGE OF LIFE CYCLE OF NEIGHBORHOOD: ☐ GROWTH ☒ EQUILIBRIUM ☐ DECLINE

% BUILT UP: *98%* GROWTH RATE: ☐ RAPID ☐ SLOW ☒ STEADY

AVERAGE MARKETING TIME: *5 mos.* PROPERTY VALUES: ☒ INCREASING ☐ DECREASING ☐ STABLE

SUPPLY/DEMAND: ☐ OVERSUPPLY ☐ UNDERSUPPLY ☒ BALANCED

CHANGE IN PRESENT LAND USE: *none anticipated*

POPULATION: ☐ INCREASING ☐ DECREASING ☒ STABLE AVERAGE FAMILY SIZE: *4*

AVERAGE FAMILY INCOME: *$30,000 to $40,000* INCOME LEVEL: ☒ INCREASING ☐ DECREASING

PREDOMINANT OCCUPATIONS: *white-collar, self-employed business people*

TYPICAL PROPERTIES:	% OF	AGE	PRICE RANGE	% OWNER OCCUPIED	% RENTALS
VACANT LOTS	*2*				
SINGLE-FAMILY RESIDENCES	*98*	*10 yrs.*	*$105,000 - $135,000*	*97*	*3*
2–6-UNIT APARTMENTS	*0*				
OVER 6-UNIT APARTMENTS	*0*				
NONRESIDENTIAL PROPERTIES	*0*				

TAX RATE: *$6 per $100 assessed value* ☐ HIGHER ☐ LOWER ☒ SAME AS COMPETING AREAS

SPECIAL ASSESSMENTS OUTSTANDING: *none*   EXPECTED: *none*

SERVICES: ☒ POLICE ☒ FIRE ☒ GARBAGE COLLECTION   OTHER: _____

DISTANCE AND DIRECTION FROM

BUSINESS AREA: *within 3 miles*

COMMERCIAL AREA: *within 1 mile*

PUBLIC ELEMENTARY AND HIGH SCHOOLS: *both within ½ mile*

PRIVATE ELEMENTARY AND HIGH SCHOOLS: *elementary, 2 miles; high school, 1 mile*

RECREATIONAL AND CULTURAL AREAS: *within 3 miles*

CHURCHES AND SYNAGOGUES: *Catholic, Lutheran, Presbyterian, Jewish synagogue*

EXPRESSWAY INTERCHANGE: *within 3 miles, in business area*

PUBLIC TRANSPORTATION: *bus — good service*

TIME TO REACH BUSINESS AREA: *15 min.*   COMMERCIAL AREA: *5 min.*

EMERGENCY MEDICAL SERVICE: *20 min.*

GENERAL TRAFFIC CONDITIONS: *good*

PROXIMITY TO HAZARDS (AIRPORT, CHEMICAL STORAGE, ETC.): *none nearby*

PROXIMITY TO NUISANCES (SMOKE, NOISE, ETC.): *none nearby*

FIGURE 6.2 Subdivision Map

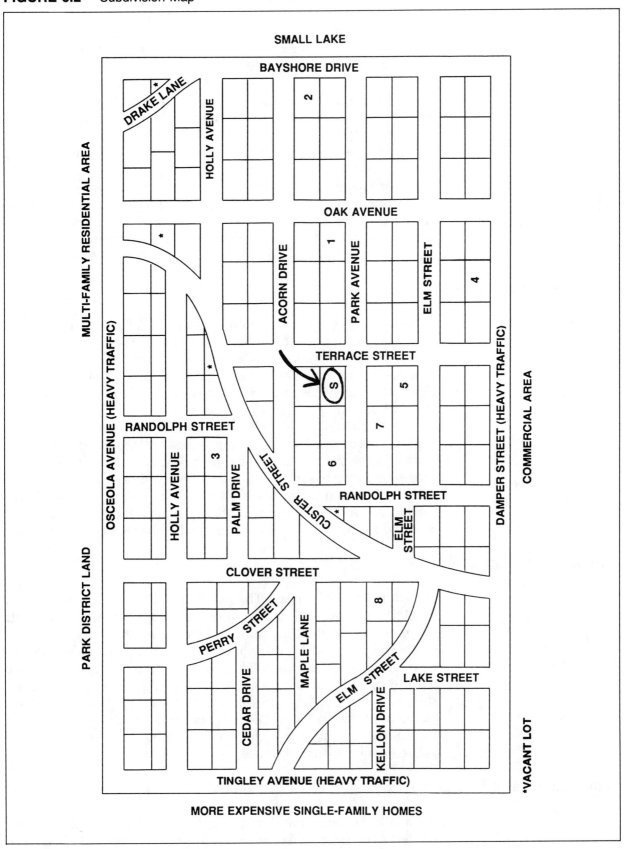

2. Equilibrium—a period of stability when new building has virtually stopped and houses in the neighborhood are usually at their highest monetary level.
3. Decline—the neighborhood enters a period of diminishing value and desirability.

These stages obviously take a long time to develop and may be followed by renewal and rehabilitation, at which point the cycle tends to repeat.

The lots on the subdivision map marked with an asterisk are vacant. New building has practically stopped, indicating that this neighborhood is, perhaps, in the stage of equilibrium.

To complete a neighborhood data form, appraisers use a number of different sources. These may include the appraiser's own files, county or city records, brokers, banks, lawyers, homeowners, merchants, published records and field observations.

Site Data and Analysis

After all the background data on the neighborhood have been gathered, the appraiser can begin to collect information about the property under appraisal. To estimate the value of improved real estate, the appraiser gathers and analyzes data on each of the two physical components of the property—the site and the house. The site will be examined first.

The rectangular lot is 80 by 150 feet—a typical size in the neighborhood. The lot slopes gently toward the street. It is evident that the owner has spent a good deal of time on landscaping, resulting in a pleasant balance between trees and bushes.

All important information about the site is recorded on a form such as the one shown in Figure 6.3. The appraiser probably had to check with a number of sources to find all of the required information.

Building Data and Analysis

House inspection is next. The exterior walls are face brick with wood trim. The roof is a simple gable type made of asphalt shingles with gutters all around. Once the exterior of the house has been examined, an interior inspection must be made. A room-by-room analysis can be conducted most systematically by using a building data form such as the one in Figure 6.4. Remember, the appraiser will have to select and screen comparable properties to apply the sales comparison approach. Accuracy will depend to a large extent, therefore, on how diligently information is gathered on the subject house.

Comparable Sales Data and Analysis

With all the pertinent background information on the subject property and its neighborhood, the appraiser is ready to begin the

FIGURE 6.3   Site Data Form

SITE DATA FORM

ADDRESS: _155 Terrace Street, Anytown, USA_

LEGAL DESCRIPTION: _Lot 15, Pine Valley Estates, Section 10_

DIMENSIONS: _80' X 150'_

SHAPE: _rectangular_   SQUARE FEET: _12,000_

TOPOGRAPHY: _level-slopes to street_ VIEW: _street-typical_

NATURAL HAZARDS: _none_

☐ INSIDE LOT   ☒ CORNER LOT   ☐ FRONTAGE: _80'_

ZONING: _Residential_   ADJACENT AREAS: _Other residential_

UTILITIES: ☒ ELECTRICITY   ☒ GAS   ☒ WATER   ☒ TELEPHONE

☒ SANITARY SEWER   ☒ STORM SEWER

IMPROVEMENTS: DRIVEWAY: _asphalt_   STREET: _asphalt_

SIDEWALK: _concrete_   CURB/GUTTER: _concrete_   ALLEY: _none_

STREETLIGHTS: _yes_

LANDSCAPING: _well done with balance between trees and bushes_

TOPSOIL: _good_   DRAINAGE: _good_

EASEMENTS: _easement running across rear 12 ft. of property_

DEED RESTRICTIONS: _10 ft. to side property lines; 35 ft. to street; 60 ft. to_

SITE PLAT: _rear property line._

See attached Subdivision Map.

most critical part of the appraisal—gathering comparable sales data to use in applying the sales comparison approach.

A comparable property must meet three conditions:

1. It must be reasonably similar to the subject property. This simply means that detailed site and building data on the comp is collected so that the relevant features of the subject property can be compared with the same features of the comp.
2. A comp must be a relatively current sale. A sale made a year or two before the appraisal most likely will not reflect current market value.
3. The sale must be an arm's-length transaction. This means that:

    *   The property was offered for sale on the open market;
    *   There was a reasonable time allowed to sell;
    *   The buyer and seller both acted with knowledge; and
    *   No pressure was brought by either party to the sale.

A number of good sources are available for obtaining data on sales of comparable properties. First, of course, are the records in the appraiser's own office. Next are the official records of deeds in the county clerk's or assessor's office. These deeds list the parties to the sale, date of sale, size and location of the site and any encumbrances. Of particular value are the real property transfer affidavits when they are available. The brokers, salespeople and lawyers who were involved in the sale are other sources of information. Professional appraisers try to establish good working relationships with these people because often they can supply information routinely that will make the appraiser's job easier. A fourth source may be either of the principals to the sale. The buyer and/or seller can tell you not only the price paid for the house, but also any firsthand information about the motives or special considerations surrounding the sale. For example, a person anticipating a foreclosure might sell a property for less than he or she would under normal circumstances. The selling price in such a case would not reflect the true market value. Published records of sales provide a fifth source. Sales data listed in newspapers frequently are unreliable, however, and must be viewed with caution.

In any list of sales that is prepared, it is likely that several sales will have to be eliminated. Following are some of the more common reasons for rejecting a sale:

1. The sale was a foreclosure.
2. The parties to the sale were related individuals or corporations.
3. Either party was under some compulsion to enter into the sale.
4. The sale was made to liquidate assets for estate-tax purposes.
5. The sale was affected by exceptional terms, either all cash or little or no cash.

FIGURE 6.4 Building Data Form

BUILDING DATA FORM

ADDRESS: *155 Terrace Street*

NO. OF UNITS: *1*   NO. OF STORIES: *1*   ORIENTATION: N S Ⓔ W

TYPE: *Single-family* DESIGN: *Ranch*   AGE: *10 years* SQUARE FEET: *1,800*

	GOOD	AVERAGE	FAIR	POOR
GENERAL CONDITION OF EXTERIOR	✓			
FOUNDATION TYPE *conc.* (BSMT.)/CRAWL SP./SLAB	✓			
EXTERIOR WALLS: (BRICK)/BLOCK/VENEER/STUCCO/	✓			
WOOD/ALUMINUM/VINYL				
WINDOW FRAMES: METAL/(WOOD)	✓			
STORM WINDOWS: *alum.* SCREENS: *alum.*	✓			
GARAGE: *brick* (ATTACHED)/DETACHED	✓			
NUMBER OF CARS: *2*				
☐ PORCH ☐ DECK ☐ PATIO ☐ SHED				
OTHER _____				
GENERAL CONDITION OF INTERIOR	✓			
INTERIOR WALLS: (DRY WALL)/PLASTER/WOOD	✓			
CEILINGS: *drywall*	✓			
FLOORS: (WOOD)/CONCRETE/(TILE)/(CARPET)	✓			
ELECTRICAL WIRING AND SERVICE: *220 volt*	✓			
HEATING PLANT: *forced-air* AGE: *10 yrs*				
(GAS)/OIL/WOOD/ELECTRIC	✓			
CENTRAL AIR-CONDITIONING: *yes* AIR FILTRATION: ___	✓			
NUMBER OF FIREPLACES: *1* TYPE: *masonry*	✓			
OTHER _____				
BATHROOM: FLOOR *cer. tile* WALLS *cer. tile paint* FIXTURES *vanity, tub shower, toilet*	✓			
BATHROOM: FLOOR *same* WALLS *same* FIXTURES *same as above*	✓			
BATHROOM: FLOOR ___ WALLS ___ FIXTURES ___	✓			
KITCHEN: FLOOR *vinyl tile* WALLS ___ CABINETS *wood*	✓			
FIXTURES *double stainless steel sink, ref., dishwasher, range w/ hood + exhaust.*	✓			

ROOM SIZES	LIVING ROOM	DINING ROOM	KITCHEN	BEDROOM	BATH	CLOSETS	FAMILY ROOM
BASEMENT							
1ST FLOOR	15' x 18'	12' x 16'	12' x 18'	10' x 12' 12' x 16'	6' x 9' 7' x 10'	4' x 8' 4' x 8'	20' x 25'
2ND FLOOR				14' x 20'		3' x 6' 2' x 5'	
ATTIC						2' x 8'	

DEPRECIATION (DESCRIBE):

PHYSICAL DETERIORATION *House is 10 years old; normal wear and tear.*

FUNCTIONAL OBSOLESCENCE *None*

EXTERNAL OBSOLESCENCE *None*

6. The sale was noncurrent. Sales made several years before the appraisal should not be used unless they are the only ones available, or unless property values have undergone little or no change.

7. The sale was not an arm's-length transaction for any reason at all.

A sale made under any of these conditions may not reflect the true market value. The important thing to remember is that if you are doubtful about the validity of a sale, *for any reason,* eliminate it from your list of sales.

Comparison Chart.   The Comparable Sales Chart in Figure 6.5 lists the common significant property variables that warrant price adjustments. The chart provides space to describe the subject property and its comparables and space to adjust the sales price of each comparable to account for significant property differences.

The subject property and each comparable should be identified by street address. The proximity of each comparable to the subject property also should be noted to determine whether a value adjustment will be made for location. The sales price of each comparable, as well as the source of the market data used, should be recorded. The easiest way to complete the chart is to describe all the details of the subject property, then do the same for each comparable in turn.

The categories listed on the Comparable Sales Chart under "Value Adjustments" produce the greatest effect on value in standard residential appraisals.

- *Sales or financing concessions.* Describe any financing arrangements such as mortgage assumptions, buydowns, installment sales contracts and wraparound loans that may have affected the sales price of a comparable property.
- *Adjusted value.* Add or subtract any difference in value warranted by changes in the market since the sale of the comparable property.
- *Date of sale.* An adjustment probably will be necessary for a sale made six months or more before the date of the appraisal.
- *Location.* The comparable property should be in the same neighborhood as the subject property. (The appraiser may have no recourse except to use properties outside the immediate area if few sales have been made in the neighborhood or if the subject property is in a rural area.) Within the same neighborhood, locations can offer significant variances, such as proximity to different land uses or frontage on a heavily traveled street. A property located across the street from a park would tend to be more valuable than one situated across the street from a gas station.

- *Site/view.* The size of the lot should be given and the site rated as good, average, fair or poor on the basis of physical features as well as on view.

  Site adjustments may reflect differences in size, shape, topography, landscaping, drainage, streets, sidewalks or other features. Except for irregularities that would make parts of a lot unusable, impair privacy or restrict on-site parking, differences in street frontage and total square footage are the most important considerations. Trees and other plantings should be of the same maturity as those of the subject property and of approximately the same quantity and quality.

  In most neighborhoods, view adjustments are uncommon; however, adjustments for houses with water or mountain views may be very substantial.

- *Design and appeal.* The style of a house probably should follow the rule of conformity; that is, the design should be compatible with that of others in the neighborhood.

- *Quality of construction.* If not the same as or equivalent to the subject property, the quality of construction of the comp will be a major adjustment. Available comparables within a particular builder's subdivision typically will be of the same construction quality. Building-cost estimating guides, published to assist builders (and appraisers, as you will learn in Chapter 8, "The Cost Approach"), can be used to rate construction quality as low, average, good or very good to excellent.

- *Age.* Because most subdivisions are completed within a relatively short period of time, there probably will be no significant differences among comparables. A brand-new home would likely be valued by the builder according to actual costs, overhead and profit. With older homes in good general condition, an age difference of five years in either direction usually is not significant. Overall upkeep is of greater importance, although the age of the house may alert the appraiser to look for outmoded design or fixtures or any needed repairs.

- *Condition.* The overall condition of each property will be noted as good, average, fair or poor. An adjustment would be indicated if the comparable is in better or worse condition than the subject property is.

- *Above-grade room count.* The total number of rooms in the house, excluding bathrooms and any basement (below-grade) rooms, is listed here. The number of bedrooms and baths and the total above-grade square footage also are noted. A major adjustment would be needed if the subject property had fewer than three bedrooms and the comparables had at least three, or vice versa. The total number of full baths (sink, toilet and tub or shower) and half-baths (sink and toilet) are tallied in this category. Modern plumbing is assumed, with an adjustment made for out-of-date fixtures.

- *Basement and finished rooms below grade.* The appraiser should note any below-grade improvements, such as a finished basement.

FIGURE 6.5   Comparable Sales Chart

	SUBJECT	COMPARABLE NO. 1	COMPARABLE NO. 2	COMPARABLE NO. 3	COMPARABLE NO. 4	COMPARABLE NO. 5
Address	155 Terrace Street	167 Oak Ave.	190 Bayshore Dr.	205 Randolph St.	500 Damper St.	127 Terrace St.
Proximity to Subject		within half-mile	within half-mile	within half-mile	within half-mile	same street
Sales Price		$110,000	$124,400	$111,500	$100,600	$114,000
Data Source	owner	sales agent	sales agent	sales agent	sales agent	sales agent
VALUE ADJUSTMENTS	DESCRIPTION	DESCRIPTION / +(-)$ Adjustment	DESCRIPTION / +(-)$ Adjustment	DESCRIPTION / +(-)$ Adjustment	DESCRIPTION / +(-)$ Adjustment	DESCRIPTION / +(-)$ Adjustment
Sales or Financing Concessions	NA	none / $	none / $	none / $	none / $	none / $
Adjusted Value						
Date of Sale/Time	NA	1 yr. ago / +4,600	2 mos. ago	4 mos. ago	3 mos. ago	1 mo. ago
Adjusted Value						
Location	quiet st.	quiet st.	facing lake / -10,000	quiet st.	heavy traffic / +5,900	quiet st.
Site/View	80'X150' good	75'X150' good	85'X155' good	80'X150' good	75'X145' poor *	80'x150' gd.
Design and Appeal	Ranch/good	Ranch/good	Ranch/good	Ranch/good	Ranch/good	Ranch/good
Quality of Construction	Brick/good	Brick/good	Brick/good	Brick/good	Brick/good	Brick/good
Age	10 yrs.	11 yrs.	10 yrs.	11 yrs.	10 yrs.	10 yrs.
Condition	good	good	good	good	good	good
Above Grade Room Count (Total / Bdrms / Baths)	7 / 3 / 2	7 / 3 / 2	7 / 3 / 2	7 / 3 / 2	7 / 3 / 2½ / -2,700	7 / 3 / 2
Gross Living Area	1,800 Sq. Ft.	1,775 Sq. Ft.	1,900 Sq. Ft.	1,750 Sq. Ft.	1,850 Sq. Ft.	1,800 Sq. Ft.
Basement & Finished Rooms Below Grade	full basement	full basement	full basement	full basement	full basement	full basement
Functional Utility	adequate	adequate	adequate	adequate	adequate	adequate
Heating/Cooling	central H/A	central H/A	central H/A	no air / +2,200	no air / +2,000	central H/A
Garage/Carport	2-car att.	2-car att.	2-car att.	2-car att.	2-car att.	2-car att.
Other Ext. Improvements	none	none	none	none	none	none
Special Energy Efficient Items	none	none	none	none	none	none
Fireplace(s)	yes/1	yes/1	yes/1	yes/1	yes/1	yes/1
Other Int. Improvements	none	none	none	none	none	none
Add'l Adj.		☒+ ☐- $4,600	☐+ ☒- $10,000	☒+ ☐- $2,200	☒+ ☐- $5,200	☐+ ☐- -0-
Adjusted Value		$114,600	$114,400	$113,700	$105,200	$114,600

*The undesirable view of comp 4 is reflected in the adjustment for location. NOTE: All adjustments are rounded to the nearest $100.

FIGURE 6.5   Comparable Sales Chart (Continued)

	SUBJECT	COMPARABLE NO. 6	COMPARABLE NO. 7	COMPARABLE NO. 8	COMPARABLE NO. 9	COMPARABLE NO. 10
Address		152 Randolph St.	250 Park Ave.	325 Clover St.		
Proximity to Subject						
Sales Price		$119,000	$109,000	$109,000	$	$
Data Source		sales agent	sales agent	sales agent		
VALUE ADJUSTMENTS	DESCRIPTION	DESCRIPTION / +(-)$ Adjustment	DESCRIPTION / +(-)$ Adjustment	DESCRIPTION / +(-)$ Adjustment	DESCRIPTION / +(-)$ Adjustment	DESCRIPTION / +(-)$ Adjustment
Sales or Financing Concessions		none	none	none		
Adjusted Value	$	$	$	$	$	$
Date of Sale/Time		5 mos. ago	4 mos. ago	6 mos. ago		
Adjusted Value		$	$	$	$	$
Location		quiet st.	quiet st.	quiet st.		
Site/View		80'x150'/gd.	70'x155'/gd.	75'x150'/gd.		
Design and Appeal		Ranch/good	Ranch/good	Ranch/good		
Quality of Construction		Brick/good	Frame/good +3,600	Frame/good +3,600		
Age		10 yrs.	11 yrs.	11 yrs.		
Condition		good	good	good		
Above Grade Room Count (Total / Bdrms / Baths)	Total / Bdrms / Baths	7 / 3 / 2½ -3,200	7 / 3 / 2	7 / 3 / 2	Total / Bdrms / Baths	Total / Bdrms / Baths
Gross Living Area	Sq. Ft.	1,750 Sq. Ft.	1,800 Sq. Ft.	1,775 Sq. Ft.	Sq. Ft.	Sq. Ft.
Basement & Finished Rooms Below Grade		full basement	full basement	full basement		
Functional Utility		adequate	adequate	adequate		
Heating/Cooling		central H/A	central H/A	no air +2,200		
Garage/Carport		2-car att.	2-car att.	2-car att.		
Other Ext. Improvements		none	none	none		
Special Energy Efficient Items		none	none	none		
Fireplace(s)		yes/1	yes/1	yes/1		
Other Int. Improvements		none	none	none		
Add'l Adj.		□+ ☒- $3,200	☒+ □- $3,600	☒+ □- $5,800	□+ □- $	□+ □- $
Adjusted Value		$115,800	$112,600	$114,800	$	$

- *Functional utility*. The house's overall compatibility with its intended use, as defined in the marketplace, should be noted. This category includes design features, such as layout and room size, that currently are desirable.
- *Heating/cooling*. The appraiser notes the type of heating unit and air-conditioning system, if any, of the subject and the comparables.
- *Garage/carport*. If the subject property does not have a garage, any garage on a comparable property would require an adjustment. A garage on the subject property would be compared for the type of construction and size.
- *Other exterior improvements*. Porch, Arizona room, Florida room, patio, pool, deck or any other living or recreation area not part of the primary house area is included here.
- *Special energy-efficient items*. High R-factor insulation, solar heating units or other energy-conservation features should be noted. As with all price adjustments, any made for energy-conservation features should reflect how much more the market will pay for the property because of the existence of the feature.
- *Fireplace(s)*. The number and type of fireplaces should be recorded.
- *Other interior improvements*. An adjustment factor is indicated if either the subject property or one of the comparables has any other interior property improvement that adds to or subtracts from its value. Luxurious finishing, such as real wood paneling, could add to a home's value.
- *Additional adjustments*. Total the dollar amounts of the positive and negative adjustments; then enter the net value of each comparable and check the + or − box as appropriate. Very large adjustments suggest that the properties are not comparable.
- *Adjusted value*. The amount of any additional adjustment is added to or subtracted from the sales price of the comparable property to obtain an adjusted sales price. This is the appraiser's best estimate of what the comparable property would have sold for if it had possessed all the significant characteristics of the subject property.

The next several pages contain an examination of how the appraiser derived the dollar adjustment values that were applied to the comparable sales in Figure 6.5.

Adjustment Process

At this point, all the data the appraiser will need to arrive at a fair market value estimate of the subject property has been gathered. The next step is to compare properties and make adjustments where needed. Although adjustments may be made for some differences between the subject property and the comparables, most of the following factors should be similar:

- Style of house,
- Age,
- Number of rooms,
- Number of bedrooms,
- Number of bathrooms,
- Size of lot,
- Size of dwelling,
- Terms of sale,
- Type of construction and
- General condition.

Naturally, wherever differences exist, adjustments must be made to bring the comparable properties into conformity with the subject property. The major categories in which adjustments for differences must be made are:

1. *Date of sale.* An adjustment must be made if market conditions change between the date of the sale of the comparable property and the date of the appraisal. Changes in market conditions may be caused by such things as fluctuations in supply and demand, inflation and economic recession.
2. *Location.* An adjustment may be necessary to compensate for locational differences between comparables and the subject property. For example, similar properties might differ in price from neighborhood to neighborhood or even in more desirable locations within the same neighborhood.
3. *Physical features.* Physical features that may require adjustments include the age of the structure, the number of rooms, the layout of the rooms (functional utility), the square feet of living space, the exterior and interior condition, and the presence or absence of special features such as a garage, central air-conditioning, fireplace, swimming pool, energy-efficient items, etc.
4. *Terms and conditions of sale.* This consideration becomes important if a sale is not financed by a standard mortgage.

Comparable sales must be adjusted *to* the subject property. That is, the subject property is the standard against which the comparable sales are evaluated and adjusted. Thus, if a feature in the comparable property is superior to that in the subject property, a minus (−) adjustment is required to make that feature equal to that in the subject property. Conversely, if a feature in the comparable property is inferior to that in the subject property, a plus (+) adjustment is required to make the feature equal to that in the subject property.

Estimating the Dollar Value of Adjustments

The most difficult step when using the sales comparison approach is determining the dollar amount of each adjustment. The accuracy of an appraisal applying this approach depends on the appraiser's use of reliable adjustment values. The adjustment value of a property feature is not simply the cost to construct or add that feature, but what a buyer is willing to pay for it, typically a lesser amount. An estimate of market value always must consider the demands of the marketplace.

Ideally, if properties could be found that were exactly alike except for one variable, the adjustment value of that variable would be the difference in selling prices of the two properties.

EXAMPLE:

House A is very similar to House B, except that House A has an attached garage, and House B has a carport. House A sold for $120,000; House B sold for $115,000. Because the garage is the only significant difference between the two properties, its market value is the difference between the selling price of $120,000 and the selling price of $115,000, or $5,000.

This type of analysis is called **matched-pair analysis** or **paired-data analysis.** An adjustment supported by just one matched pair, as in the example, however, may be unreliable. In actual practice, the appraiser will analyze as many properties as needed to be able to isolate each significant variable and to substantiate the accuracy of an adjustment value. Most neighborhoods include very similar types of properties, so this usually is not so difficult as it may first appear to be.

The number of sales needed for an accurate estimate of market value cannot be easily specified, but the fewer the sales, the more carefully they must be investigated. If the appraiser analyzes 10 to 20 or more properties, a market pattern may be more evident and, with better documentation, the value of individual differences may be estimated fairly accurately.

Figure 6.6 is a Sales Price Adjustment Chart that has been completed for eight properties, all comparable to each other. Each relevant adjustment variable has been highlighted. Although an appraiser ordinarily will need two or more instances of each variable as a check on the accuracy of an adjustment value, for the sake of brevity only one comparable with each variable is presented here.

Because Properties A and C exhibit no variables, they will be used to define the standard against which the worth of each variable will be measured. Property A sold for $125,000, and Property C sold for $124,750. Because the selling prices are so close, $125,000 will be used as the base house value for a typical property in the neighborhood.

Now let's estimate how much each adjustment factor is worth in dollars as each one is analyzed singly.

Time Adjustment.   The time factor refers to the economic changes from the date of the sale to the date of the appraisal. To isolate the time factor, those sales that differ from each other in the date of sale only are selected. If several properties are alike except for the length of time since the date of sale, then it is logical to assume that the time factor is reflected in the difference in selling prices.

Property D was sold one year ago for $120,000 (see Figure 6.6); Property A, the base house, or standard, sold one month ago for $125,000. The adjustment value to be made in the case of a year-old sale is, therefore:

$$\$125,000 \quad - \quad \$120,000 \quad = \quad \$5,000$$

The $5,000 adjustment value can be expressed as a percentage of the total cost of the property:

$$\frac{\$5,000}{\$120,000} \quad = \quad .04166, \text{ or rounded to } 4.2\%$$

In this case, the adjustment value of the variable is $5,000. If a one-year time adjustment was required for another property, the dollar value of the adjustment would be the amount derived by applying the percentage of value to that property's sales price.

Note that the adjustment values determined through matched-pair analysis in Figure 6.6 were applied to the comparable properties used in the sample appraisal in Figure 6.5. For example, the sales price of Property 1 was adjusted by 4.2 percent ($110,000 × .042 = $4,600 rounded) because it was a year-old sale.

Location.   Property G, on a more desirable site facing a small lake, sold for $10,900 *more* than the standard; therefore, this superior location indicates an adjustment of $10,900, or approximately 8 percent.

Property B, on the other hand, fronts on a heavily traveled street and is directly across from a commercial shopping area. Property B sold for $7,000 (approximately 5.9 percent) *less* than the base value house.

Locational adjustments in the sample appraisal were required for Properties 2 and 4; thus, based on the appraiser's matched-pair analysis, the sales prices of these properties have been adjusted by 8 percent and 5.9 percent, respectively.

Physical Features.   In the sample appraisal, physical feature adjustments were made for brick versus frame siding (Properties 7 and 8), an extra half-bath (4, 6) and central air-conditioning (3, 4, 8).

Based on the matched-pair analysis in Figure 6.6, the appraiser estimated the following adjustment values:

FIGURE 6.6   Sales Price Adjustment Chart

COMPARABLES

	A	B	C	D	E	F	G	H
SALES PRICE	$125,000	$118,000	$124,750	$120,000	$121,000	$125,500	$135,900	$122,500
FINANCING	standard mortgage	standard mortgage	standard mortgage	standard mortgage	standard mortgage	standard mortgage	standard mortgage	standard mortgage
DATE OF SALE	1 mo. ago	4 mos. ago	2 mos. ago	1 yr. ago	3 mos. ago	5 mos. ago	3 mos. ago	2 mos. ago
LOCATION	quiet street	heavy traffic	quiet street	quiet street	quiet street	quiet street	facing lake	quiet street
SITE/VIEW	good	good	good	good	good	good	good	good
SIZE OF LOT	75'x125'	75'x125'	75'x125'	78'x130'	72'x135'	75'x125'	75'x125'	80'x120'
DESIGN AND APPEAL	good	good	good	good	good	good	good	good
CONSTRUCTION	brick	brick	brick	brick	frame siding	brick	brick	brick
AGE	14 yrs.	15 yrs.	14 yrs.	14 yrs.	14 yrs.	13 yrs.	14 yrs.	13 yrs.
CONDITION	good	good	good	good	good	good	good	good
NO. OF RMS./BEDRMS./BATHS	8/3/2	8/3/2	8/3/2	8/3/2	8/3/2	8/3/2½	8/3/2	8/3/2
SQ. FT. OF LIVING SPACE	1,900	1,850	1,900	1,850	1,900	1,925	1,875	1,900
OTHER SPACE (BASEMENT)	full basement	full basement	full basement	full basement	full basement	full basement	full basement	full basement
FUNCTIONAL UTILITY	adeq.	adeq.	adeq.	adeq.	adeq.	adeq.	adeq.	adeq.
HEATING/COOLING	central H/A	central H/A	central H/A	central H/A	central H/A	central H/A	central H/A	no cent. air
GARAGE/CARPORT	2-car att.	2-car att.	2-car att.	2-car att.	2-car att.	2-car att.	2-car att.	2-car att.
OTHER EXT. IMPROVEMENTS	patio	patio	patio	patio	patio	patio	patio	patio
SPECIAL ENERGY EFFICIENT ITEMS	none	none	none	none	none	none	none	none
FIREPLACE(S)	yes/1	yes/1	yes/1	yes/1	yes/1	yes/1	yes/1	yes/1
OTHER INT. IMPROVEMENTS	none	none	none	none	none	none	none	none
TYPICAL HOUSE VALUE	$125,000	$125,000	$125,000	$125,000	$125,000	$125,000	$125,000	$125,000
VARIABLE FEATURE	—	poor location	—	year-old sale	frame siding	extra half-bath	excellent location	no cent. air
ADJUSTMENT VALUE OF VARIABLE		$7,000		$5,000	$4,000	$3,500	$10,900	$2,500

brick over frame—$4,000, or approximately 3.3 percent (Property E)
extra half-bath—$3,500, or approximately 2.7 percent (Property F)
central air-conditioning—$2,500, or approximately 2 percent
(Property H)

These adjustment values then were applied to the appropriate
properties in the sample appraisal.

Value Estimate

Using the adjusted values compiled in Figure 6.5, the appraiser
can determine the appropriate estimate of market value to assign
to the subject property using the sales comparison approach.

Even when the appraiser is dealing with comparable properties that are virtually identical, however, the adjusted values
rarely will be identical. Usually, at least some differences in real
estate transactions, however minor, will cause selling prices to
vary. Whatever the reasons, the adjusted values of the comparable properties probably will not be identical.

No formula exists for reconciling the indicated values. Rather,
this involves the application of careful analysis and judgment for
which no mathematical formula can be substituted. The appraiser's task is to choose the adjusted value that seems to best reflect
the characteristics of the subject property. In other words, which
comparable is most like the subject property? The adjusted value
of that property most likely will represent the market value of
the subject property.

In the sample appraisal, the estimated value of the subject
property is $114,000. Here is how the appraiser arrived at that
conclusion.

First, the extreme was rejected—Sale 4—because of the large
number of adjustments needed. Then the top seven comparables
were ranked, which, in the appraiser's opinion, were most nearly
similar to the subject property:

Sale No.	Sales Price	Net Adjustments	Adjusted Sales Price
5	$114,000	-0-	$114,000
3	$111,500	+ $2,200	$113,700
6	$119,000	– $3,200	$115,800
2	$124,400	– $10,000	$114,400
7	$109,000	+ $3,600	$112,600
1	$110,000	+ $4,600	$114,600
8	$109,000	+ $5,800	$114,800

Because the value range is close, and because Sale 5 with no
adjustments topped the list, the appraiser felt that it was reasonable to assume that the subject property has a market value
equal to the adjusted sales price of Sale 5.

APPRAISAL WORKSHEET

1. Using the blank data forms on pages 103–5, describe the neighborhood, site and house.
2. Find three or four recent sales of houses comparable to the subject property and conduct a comparison analysis. Use the blank Comparable Sales Chart on page 106.
3. Based on your analysis, what is your best estimate of the market value range of the house? _____

NEIGHBORHOOD DATA FORM

BOUNDARIES: ADJACENT TO:

     NORTH _____

     SOUTH _____

     EAST _____

     WEST _____

TOPOGRAPHY: _____ ☐ URBAN ☐ SUBURBAN ☐ RURAL

STAGE OF LIFE CYCLE OF NEIGHBORHOOD: ☐ GROWTH ☐ EQUILIBRIUM ☐ DECLINE

% BUILT UP: _____ GROWTH RATE: ☐ RAPID ☐ SLOW ☐ STEADY

AVERAGE MARKETING TIME: _____ PROPERTY VALUES: ☐ INCREASING ☐ DECREASING ☐ STABLE

SUPPLY/DEMAND: ☐ OVERSUPPLY ☐ UNDERSUPPLY ☐ BALANCED

CHANGE IN PRESENT LAND USE: _____

POPULATION: ☐ INCREASING ☐ DECREASING ☐ STABLE   AVERAGE FAMILY SIZE: _____

AVERAGE FAMILY INCOME: _____ INCOME LEVEL: ☐ INCREASING ☐ DECREASING

PREDOMINANT OCCUPATIONS: _____

TYPICAL PROPERTIES:	% OF	AGE	PRICE RANGE	% OWNER OCCUPIED	% RENTALS
VACANT LOTS					
SINGLE-FAMILY RESIDENCES					
2–6-UNIT APARTMENTS					
OVER 6-UNIT APARTMENTS					
NONRESIDENTIAL PROPERTIES					

TAX RATE: _____ ☐ HIGHER ☐ LOWER ☐ SAME AS COMPETING AREAS

SPECIAL ASSESSMENTS OUTSTANDING: _____ EXPECTED: _____

SERVICES: ☐ POLICE ☐ FIRE ☐ GARBAGE COLLECTION   OTHER: _____

DISTANCE AND DIRECTION FROM

     BUSINESS AREA: _____

     COMMERCIAL AREA: _____

     PUBLIC ELEMENTARY AND HIGH SCHOOLS: _____

     PRIVATE ELEMENTARY AND HIGH SCHOOLS: _____

     RECREATIONAL AND CULTURAL AREAS: _____

     CHURCHES AND SYNAGOGUES: _____

     EXPRESSWAY INTERCHANGE: _____

     PUBLIC TRANSPORTATION: _____

       TIME TO REACH BUSINESS AREA: _____ COMMERCIAL AREA: _____

     EMERGENCY MEDICAL SERVICE: _____

GENERAL TRAFFIC CONDITIONS: _____

PROXIMITY TO HAZARDS (AIRPORT, CHEMICAL STORAGE, ETC.): _____

PROXIMITY TO NUISANCES (SMOKE, NOISE, ETC.): _____

SITE DATA FORM

ADDRESS: _____

LEGAL DESCRIPTION: _____

_____

_____

_____

_____

_____

DIMENSIONS: _____

SHAPE: _____   SQUARE FEET: _____

TOPOGRAPHY: _____   VIEW: _____

NATURAL HAZARDS: _____

☐ INSIDE LOT   ☐ CORNER LOT   ☐ FRONTAGE: _____

ZONING: _____   ADJACENT AREAS: _____

UTILITIES: ☐ ELECTRICITY   ☐ GAS   ☐ WATER   ☐ TELEPHONE

☐ SANITARY SEWER   ☐ STORM SEWER

IMPROVEMENTS: DRIVEWAY: _____   STREET: _____

SIDEWALK: _____   CURB/GUTTER: _____   ALLEY: _____

STREETLIGHTS: _____

LANDSCAPING: _____

TOPSOIL: _____   DRAINAGE: _____

EASEMENTS: _____

DEED RESTRICTIONS: _____

SITE PLAT:

BUILDING DATA FORM

ADDRESS: _____

NO. OF UNITS: _____ NO. OF STORIES: _____ ORIENTATION: N S E W

TYPE: _____ DESIGN: _____ AGE: _____ SQUARE FEET: _____

	GOOD	AVERAGE	FAIR	POOR
GENERAL CONDITION OF EXTERIOR				
FOUNDATION TYPE _____ BSMT./CRAWL SP./SLAB				
EXTERIOR WALLS: BRICK/BLOCK/VENEER/STUCCO/				
WOOD/ALUMINUM/VINYL				
WINDOW FRAMES: METAL/WOOD				
STORM WINDOWS: ____ SCREENS: ____				
GARAGE: _____ ATTACHED/DETACHED				
NUMBER OF CARS: ____				
☐ PORCH ☐ DECK ☐ PATIO ☐ SHED				
OTHER _____				
GENERAL CONDITION OF INTERIOR				
INTERIOR WALLS: DRY WALL/PLASTER/WOOD				
CEILINGS: _____				
FLOORS: WOOD/CONCRETE/TILE/CARPET				
ELECTRICAL WIRING AND SERVICE: _____				
HEATING PLANT: _____ AGE: _____				
GAS/OIL/WOOD/ELECTRIC				
CENTRAL AIR-CONDITIONING: _____ AIR FILTRATION: ___				
NUMBER OF FIREPLACES: _____ TYPE: _____				
OTHER _____				
BATHROOM: FLOOR___WALLS_____FIXTURES _____				
BATHROOM: FLOOR___WALLS_____FIXTURES _____				
BATHROOM: FLOOR___WALLS_____FIXTURES _____				
KITCHEN: FLOOR___WALLS_____CABINETS _____				
FIXTURES _____				

ROOM SIZES	LIVING ROOM	DINING ROOM	KITCHEN	BEDROOM	BATH	CLOSETS	FAMILY ROOM
BASEMENT							
1ST FLOOR							
2ND FLOOR							
ATTIC							

DEPRECIATION (DESCRIBE):

PHYSICAL DETERIORATION _____

FUNCTIONAL OBSOLESCENCE _____

EXTERNAL OBSOLESCENCE _____

COMPARABLE SALES CHART

	SUBJECT	COMPARABLE NO. 1		COMPARABLE NO. 2		COMPARABLE NO. 3		COMPARABLE NO. 4		COMPARABLE NO. 5	
Address											
Proximity to Subject											
Sales Price		$		$		$		$		$	
Data Source											
VALUE ADJUSTMENTS	DESCRIPTION	DESCRIPTION	+(−)$ Adjustment	DESCRIPTION	+(−)$ Adjustment	DESCRIPTION	+(−)$ Adjustment	DESCRIPTION	+(−)$ Adjustment	DESCRIPTION	+(−)$ Adjustment
Sales or Financing Concessions											
Adjusted Value		$		$		$		$		$	
Date of Sale/Time											
Adjusted Value		$		$		$		$		$	
Location											
Site/View											
Design and Appeal											
Quality of Construction											
Age											
Condition											
Above Grade Room Count	Total Bdrms Baths	Total Bdrms Baths		Total Bdrms Baths		Total Bdrms Baths		Total Bdrms Baths		Total Bdrms Baths	
Gross Living Area	Sq. Ft.	Sq. Ft.		Sq. Ft.		Sq. Ft.		Sq. Ft.		Sq. Ft.	
Basement & Finished Rooms Below Grade											
Functional Utility											
Heating/Cooling											
Garage/Carport											
Other Ext. Improvements											
Special Energy Efficient Items											
Fireplace(s)											
Other Int. Improvements											
Add'l Adj.		□+ □− $		□+ □− $		□+ □− $		□+ □− $		□+ □− $	
Adjusted Value		$		$		$		$		$	

7

Site Valuation

Much of the information discussed in this chapter already should be familiar to you, although you may not have thought about it in exactly the way that it is discussed here. To illustrate, let's start with an example.

EXAMPLE:

A three-bedroom, two-bathroom house with an attached two-car garage is constructed on a suburban building lot in Twelve Oaks, Anystate. At the same time, an exact duplicate of the house is constructed by the same builder on a lot of the same size and topography in the neighboring town of Three Maples. The same kinds of materials are used, the same craftspeople are hired to perform the work and both houses are fitted with the same brand of appliances. Yet, the asking price for the house in Twelve Oaks is $185,000, and the asking price for the house in Three Maples is $175,000. Why is there a price differential? In this case, the answer lies in the value of the two parcels of land on which the houses were built. The lot in Twelve Oaks cost the builder $50,000, while the lot in Three Maples cost the builder only $40,000.

Most people who have shopped for a house have heard the old maxim that the three most important factors that contribute to property value are location, location and location. As much of a cliché as that concept may seem, it reflects two basic facts that affect all real estate appraisals:

1.   Land value is the primary determinant of overall real estate value and
2.   Land value is determined by market demand.

The most luxurious building constructed with the finest materials and the greatest attention to detail, regardless of its construction cost, will be only as valuable as the demand for that kind of property *in that location* warrants. As explained in the first few chapters of this book, market demand is a reflection of the number of possible buyers competing for the available products and services. The number of buyers and sellers in the marketplace for real estate is subject to many variables, including the same factors that affect the country's overall economy, such as income and employment levels. The real estate appraiser's job is to identify the market variables that affect land value as well as possible and to determine their impact on value.

This chapter discusses the basic principles and techniques that enable an appraiser to estimate the market value of land after identifying, gathering and analyzing the necessary data.

SEPARATE SITE VALUATIONS

Although vacant land can be appraised, most land valuations consider the property's value as a building site. A **site** is land that has been prepared for its intended use by the addition of such improvements as grading, utilities and road access. These improvements do not include structures, even though the same term can be used to apply to both. A site, then, is land that is ready for building or that already has a building on it but is being valued separately from the building.

Cost Approach

One of the primary reasons for a separate site valuation is to use the cost approach to value. The formula for the cost approach is:

$$\begin{array}{c} \text{Reproduction or} \\ \text{Replacement} \\ \text{Cost of Improvement(s)} \end{array} - \begin{array}{c} \text{Accrued} \\ \text{Depreciation} \end{array} + \text{Site Value} = \begin{array}{c} \text{Property} \\ \text{Value} \end{array}$$

Even though the elements of site preparation, such as access and utilities, are improvements to the land, in the cost approach formula the term *improvements* refers to structures. An appraiser using the cost approach will calculate the value of the land separately and then add that value to the depreciated construction cost of the structures. The cost approach is covered in detail in Chapter 8.

Assessments and Taxation

Local communities frequently assess individual property owners for the cost of installation or upkeep of utilities and roads that benefit their property. The amount of the individual assessment typically is based on the value of the site, exclusive of any structures.

Real property taxes generally are *ad valorem* taxes; that is, they are based on a percentage of property value. Most states require separate valuations of site and structures when determining the property value base to which the property tax rate will be applied.

Structures owned for investment purposes can be depreciated. Their value can be deducted from income produced by the investment over the term allowed by the applicable federal income tax law provision. Because land is *not* considered a wasting asset, its value must be subtracted from the overall property value before the amount of the allowable deduction can be calculated.

Income Capitalization

Using the income capitalization approach to appraising, the appraiser must determine the present value of the right to receive the income stream estimated to be produced by the property that is the subject of the appraisal. One of the methods that relies on income data to determine value is the **building residual technique,** which requires the appraiser to find land value separately. The appraiser subtracts an appropriate return on land value from the net income produced by the property to indicate the income available to the building.

Highest and Best Use

A highest and best use study can be a very complex process. If the appraiser is asked to consider the entire range of uses to which the property could be put, he or she must consider the value of the land separately from the value of any particular structure that can be erected on it. The property will be valued both with and without structures. The appraiser will consider not only the most valuable present and prospective use of the site, but also whether a zoning change or other approval necessary for a particular use is likely.

Condemnation Appraisals

When land is condemned for a public or quasi-public purpose, courts frequently will require separate site and building valuations as part of the determination of the property's fair market value.

FIGURE 7.1   Metes and Bounds Legal Description

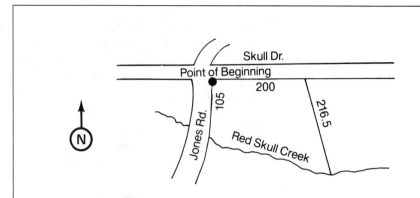

A tract of land located in Red Skull, Virginia, described as follows: Beginning at the intersection of the east line of Jones Road and the south line of Skull Drive; thence east along the south line of Skull Drive 200 feet; thence south 15° east 216.5 feet, more or less, to the center thread of Red Skull Creek; thence northwesterly along the center line of said creek to its intersection with the east line of Jones Road; thence north 105 feet, more or less, along the east line of Jones Road to the point of beginning.

Source: Fillmore W. Galaty, Wellington J. Allaway and Robert C. Kyle, *Modern Real Estate Practice,* Twelfth Edition (Chicago: Real Estate Education Company, 1991), p. 88.

SITE DATA

The appraiser performing a site appraisal must determine and then collect the necessary data.

Identification

The first step in site analysis is to identify the property. If you have ever heard one of the horror stories about a house built on the wrong subdivision lot, you know the importance of identifying the correct parcel, and how easily an error can be made. The appraiser should have a complete and accurate legal description of the entire parcel, as well as its street address, if any. The appraisal report should include maps showing the property's boundaries as well as its location in the neighborhood.

Three major methods of legal description of land are used in the United States.

Metes and Bounds System.   One of the oldest methods of legal description is the **metes and bounds system.** A parcel of land is described by reference to measured distances, called **metes,** from a stated **point of beginning** to **monuments** or **markers.** Individual markers can be either natural (a large rock or tree) or human-made (a fence post). Figure 7.1 is an example of an early metes and bounds legal description.

Because markers often were removed or destroyed, the need for a more accurate and reliable method of legal description soon became apparent.

FIGURE 7.2   Principal Meridians and Baselines

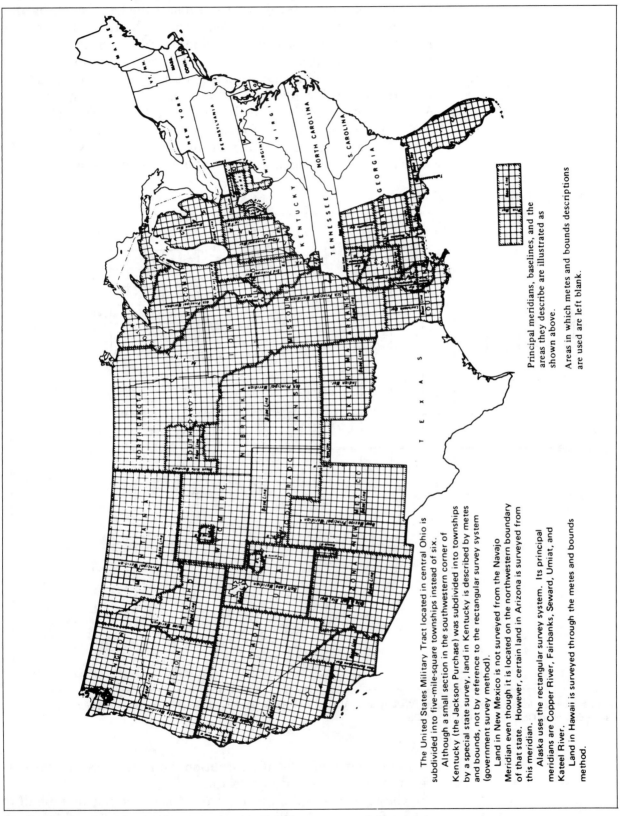

The United States Military Tract located in central Ohio is subdivided into five-mile-square townships instead of six.

Although a small section in the southwestern corner of Kentucky (the Jackson Purchase) was subdivided into townships by a special state survey, land in Kentucky is described by metes and bounds, not by reference to the rectangular survey system (government survey method).

Land in New Mexico is not surveyed from the Navajo Meridian even though it is located on the northwestern boundary of that state. However, certain land in Arizona is surveyed from this meridian.

Alaska uses the rectangular survey system. Its principal meridians are Copper River, Fairbanks, Seward, Umiat, and Kateel River.

Land in Hawaii is surveyed through the metes and bounds method.

Principal meridians, baselines, and the areas they describe are illustrated as shown above.

Areas in which metes and bounds descriptions are used are left blank.

Source: Fillmore W. Galaty, Wellington J. Allaway and Robert C. Kyle, *Modern Real Estate Practice*, Twelfth Edition (Chicago: Real Estate Education Company, 1991), p. 87.

Rectangular Survey System. In 1785, Congress established the **government survey system,** also called the **rectangular survey system.** Using this system, land is identified by reference to one of the sets of principal meridians and baselines designated throughout the country, as shown in the map in Figure 7.2.

Distances from the intersection of a principal meridian and baseline are measured by reference to townships of six miles square. Rows of townships are counted north or south in tiers from the baseline and east or west in ranges from the principal meridian, as shown in the left side of Figure 7.3. Each township is further divided into 36 sections of 640 acres apiece, as shown in the right side of Figure 7.3.

FIGURE 7.3   Townships and Sections

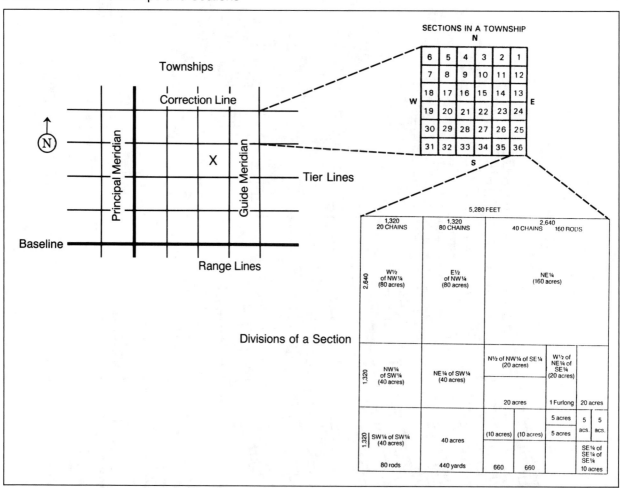

Source: Adapted from Fillmore W. Galaty, Wellington J. Allaway and Robert C. Kyle, *Modern Real Estate Practice* (Chicago: Real Estate Education Company, 1991), pp. 91, 93.

An example of a legal description using the rectangular survey system is shown in Figure 7.4.

The legal description in Figure 7.4 is of the north one-half of the southwest one-fourth of Section 17, Grenadier Township, which is located in tier 3 north and range 5 east of the intersection of

FIGURE 7.4   Rectangular Survey System Description

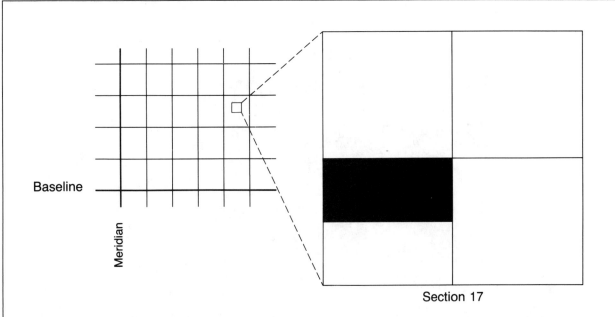

Baseline

Meridian

Section 17

The N ½ of the SW ¼ of Section 17, Grenadier Township, T3N R5E of the Washington Meridian and Baseline.

the Washington meridian and baseline. The parcel described is 80 acres (½ × ¼ × 640 acres).

Rectangular survey system descriptions most often are used to describe large tracts of land and rural property. This system is used in most states, with the exceptions noted in Figure 7.2.

Lot and Block System.   Today, most urban and suburban real estate can be referred to by a **lot and block** description. The lot and block numbers refer to a particular tract shown in a subdivision map on file in the county recorder's office. Figure 7.5 is an example of a legal description using a **tract map,** also called a **plat map,** which has been divided into lots and blocks.

Analysis

Once the subject property has been identified adequately, it must be analyzed in detail. In addition to general information on economic trends and factors influencing value, the appraiser will need data on property features and other facts, including:

- Size of the site;
- Boundaries;
- Topography;
- Location of the site in terms of position on the block;
- Utilities and other site improvements;

FIGURE 7.5   Lot and Block Description

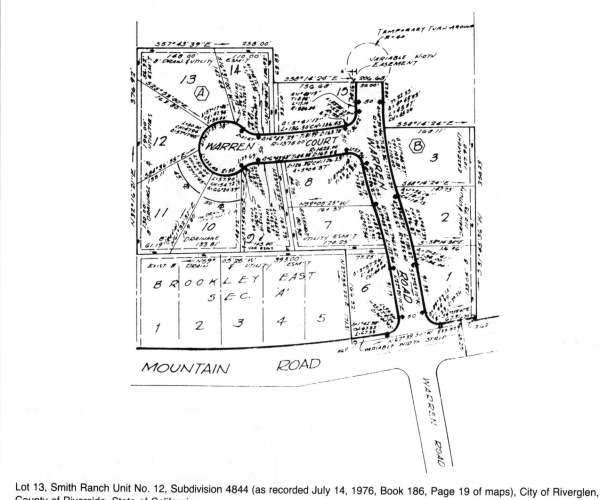

Lot 13, Smith Ranch Unit No. 12, Subdivision 4844 (as recorded July 14, 1976, Book 186, Page 19 of maps), City of Riverglen, County of Riverside, State of California.

Source: Charles O. Stapleton III, Thomas J. Moran and Martha R. Williams, *California Real Estate Principles* (Chicago: Real Estate Education Company, 1987), p. 17.

- Soil composition, especially as related to grading, septic system or bearing capacity for foundations;
- Zoning of the subject property and surrounding properties;
- Easements, deed restrictions or publicly held rights-of-way; and
- Any limitations on the use of the site for building purposes.

With all of this information collected and studied, the appraiser is ready to apply one of the following site valuation methods.

METHODS OF SITE VALUATION

Five valuation methods are commonly used when appraising building sites. Two of them, the **land residual method** and **ground rent capitalization method,** will not be discussed because they generally are used only for commercial properties and require complex calculations of income and lease payments. Following is an explanation of the other three land valuation methods, which are used to appraise various kinds of residential real estate.

Sales Comparison Method

Using the **sales comparison method,** sales of similar vacant sites are analyzed and compared. After any necessary adjustments to sales prices are made, the appraiser derives an estimate of value for the subject site. No significant differences exist between the data valuation of improved properties (those with structures) and unimproved sites. Because the sales comparison approach is covered in detail in Chapter 6, it is simply reviewed here.

Of all the methods of site valuation, the sales comparison method generally provides the most reliable indicator of market value. The appraiser's objective is to determine the most probable value of the subject property by interpreting data from sales of similar properties. The appraiser's first task in applying this method is to find sales data on comparable properties. Because no two parcels of land are ever identical, an appraiser always will have to compensate for some differences when comparing sales properties to the subject property. Typical differences include:

- Location (block, neighborhood, area);
- Physical characteristics;
- Zoning and land-use restrictions;
- Terms of financing; and/or
- Conditions of sale.

Of course, the appraiser also is concerned that the comparable properties have been sold fairly recently. If any sale occurred more than six months before the date of the appraisal, an adjustment probably is indicated.

The adjustment process should eliminate the effect on value of the significant property differences. When adjusting the sales price of a comparable property, lump-sum dollar amounts or percentages customarily are used. Adjustments always are made to the sales price of the comparable property. If the comparable property is inferior in some respect to the subject property, its sale price is increased by an appropriate dollar amount or percentage. If the comparable property is superior in some category to the subject property, its sales price is decreased commensurately.

The appraiser uses the adjusted sales prices to determine the most likely value to assign to the subject property.

EXAMPLE:

A lot in Hilltop Estates is being appraised. Hilltop Estates is a subdivision zoned for single-family residences.

Of the original 110 lots platted, only seven remain un-improved. The subject property is located at 415 Pamela Court and is 75 by 150 feet with a gentle downhill grade. The most recent lot sales in Hilltop Estates have been those listed as follows:

	Lot A	Lot B	Lot C	Lot D
Address	316 Pamela	506 Aria	384 Paula	717 Rachel
Sales Price	$85,000	$65,000	$75,000	$95,000
Date of Sale	Two months ago	One month ago	Three months ago	Six weeks ago
Financing Concessions	None	None	None	None
Location	Same block as subject	Three blocks from subject	One block from subject	Six blocks from subject
Size	75′ × 140′	75′ × 150′	70′ × 160′	100′ × 145′
Area	10,050 sf	11,250 sf	11,200 sf	14,500 sf
Topography	Downhill	Steep uphill	Flat	Downhill
View	City	Street	Street	City
Utilities	Elect/Gas/ Phone/Cable	Elect/Gas/ Phone/Cable	Elect/Gas/ Phone/Cable	Elect/Gas/ Phone/Cable
Zoning	SF-1	SF-1	SF-1	SF-1
Other	Graded	Not graded	Graded	Graded

The appraiser makes the following adjustments to the sales prices of the comparables:

Lot A—Size, $1,500   Adjusted Value $86,500
Lot B—Topography, $5,000;
    View, $10,000;
    Grading, $5,000   Adjusted Value $85,000
Lot C—Topography, –$5,000;
    View, $10,000   Adjusted Value $80,000
Lot D—Size, –$15,000   Adjusted Value $80,000

The adjusted values range from $80,000 to $86,500. Overall, however, Lot A is most similar to the subject property. Lot B, an uphill lot, will require substantial excavation to prepare for building. Lot C, while offering the advantage of flat, buildable space, only has a view of the street and neighboring houses. Lot D is very similar to the subject property, though somewhat larger. For these reasons and because few lots are available in this desirable subdivision, the appraiser determines that $86,500 is the appropiate estimate of market value for the subject property.

In this example, the appraiser felt justified in selecting an adjusted value that was at the high end of the indicated value range. If the market conditions were not favorable and if more competing properties were on the market, the appraiser would have taken those factors into account and probably would have made a more conservative (lower) estimate.

Allocation Method

Land value may be treated as a percentage or proportion of the total value of an improved property by using the **allocation method.** Often, a consistent relationship exists between land and building values. For example, an area may tend to have a one-to-four land-to-building value ratio. This means that the building value will be four times the land value. If the total property value is $500,000, $100,000 will be allocated to the land and $400,000 to the building. This phenomenon occurs partly because developers do not want to "overimprove" a parcel with a building far in excess of what the value of the site warrants. As a rough rule of thumb, such a ratio will serve as a very broad indicator of what buyers in the marketplace are likely to expect.

As demand for buildable land increases, the ratio of land to building value tends to narrow as their relative values come closer together. The one-to-four ratio may become one-to-three or even one-to-two. This occurs because the total cost of the land and building will be limited by what buyers in the marketplace are prepared to pay, although the affordability "ceiling" will tend to rise as demand increases and supply dwindles. During the past several decades, buyers and renters of residential property have earmarked more and more of their incomes for housing.

An obvious failing of the allocation method is that it does not take into account individual property differences. This method should be relied on only when there is a lack of current data on vacant sites that are comparable to the property being appraised. It also may be useful as a broad check of an appraisal by another method.

Subdivision Development Method

The last land valuation method concerns the value of raw (undeveloped) land that is suitable for single-family residential building lots.

Residential development in and around urban areas is a fact of life and most sites suitable for single-family houses are part of subdivisions that started out as large tracts of undeveloped land. The 160-acre dairy farm that supported one or more families comfortably becomes—seemingly overnight—the center of a whirl-wind as bulldozers move in to prepare the land for homebuilding. If the present residents of the area are lucky, the farmhouse remains as a reminder of simpler times. Once the building sites are prepared and construction is ready to begin, the individual lots will be priced as the market will allow. Because the final pricing will depend to a great extent on the way in which the subdivision is platted, how can a fair value for the raw land be determined?

One method that can be used factors out the expenses of development to determine a fair market value for the land prior to development. In the **subdivision development method,** all probable costs of development, including the developer's profit and cost of financing, are subtracted from the total projected sales prices of the individual units. The figure that results is the value of the raw land.

EXAMPLE:

Happy Hollow Acres is a 40-acre farm that is being considered for subdivision development. Because the land is in the path of a new extension of the interstate highway, its current highest and best use is single-family home development. It is estimated that the property can be divided into 160 buildable lots, after allowing for roads and the open space required by the planning commission. By estimating the probable sales prices of the lots and computing the costs of development, the appraiser can determine the value of the undeveloped land.

Total projected sales:		
160 lots at $40,000 per lot		$6,400,000
Total projected development costs:		
Street grading and paving, sidewalks, curbs, gutters, sanitary and storm sewers for 160 lots at $12,000 per lot	$1,920,000	
Other costs, including sales office and commissions, estimated at a total of 20% of sales ($6,400,000 × 20%)	1,280,000	
Developer's profit, 10% of projected sales ($6,400,000 × 10%)	640,000	
Total development costs		3,840,000
Estimated value of raw land		$2,560,000
Raw land value per lot ($2,560,000 ÷ 160)		$16,000

This is a very simplified example of the kind of calculations that will take place. Because the eventual site sales would not occur for some time, the appraiser also would have to take into account the time value of the money used to purchase the raw land, whether the developer's or borrowed funds. That is, how much would the developer be willing to pay for the unimproved land, considering the interest that the developer would be losing on the funds that would buy the land, or the interest that the developer would be paying on the loan taken out for the purchase of the land?

In the Happy Hollow Acres example, the total land value was estimated at $2,560,000. It is estimated that the lot sales will take place over three years. The developer expects a yield of ten percent from the funds invested over those three years *over and above any profit from the work of development*. By applying the appropriate *reversion factor* to the dollar value of each year's anticipated sales, the *present* value of the undeveloped parcel can be estimated. The calculations are given as follows:

First year:	60 lots at $16,000 per lot = $960,000	
	$960,000 discounted to present worth at 10% for one year (.909)	$872,640
Second year:	70 lots at $16,000 per lot = $1,120,000	
	$1,120,000 discounted to present worth at 10% for two years (.826)	925,120
Third year:	30 lots at $16,000 per lot = $480,000	
	$480,000 discounted to present worth for three years (.751)	360,480
Present value of $2,560,000 discounted partially over one, two and three years		$2,158,240
Present discounted lot value		$13,489

Based on the projected costs and sales figures for this developer, the present worth of the 40 undeveloped acres is $2,158,240. Note that after taking into account the carrying charges on the development funds invested in the project, the present value of the land required for a single lot decreased from $16,000 to approximately $13,500. Again, this example is greatly simplified. The projected sales prices, for example, probably will be expected to increase over the three years that the lots are sold, which would increase the value per lot. The value of any salvageable structures already on the property also would have to be included.

APPRAISAL WORKSHEET

1. Is the home located in a subdivision? _____
2. If so, how many lots were part of the original subdivision plan? _____
3. How many undeveloped lots are in the subdivision or the immediate vicinity (say, one mile)? _____
4. List three or four recent sales of building lots comparable to the subject and describe each property.

	Lot A	Lot B	Lot C	Lot D
Address				
Sales Price				
Date of Sale				
Financing Concessions				
Location				
Size				
Area				
Topography				
View				
Utilities				
Zoning				
Other				

The Cost Approach

One approach to appraising that is especially appropriate for certain types of property is the **cost approach.** To reach an estimate of value by the cost approach, the appraiser (1) calculates the cost to reproduce or replace the existing structures; (2) subtracts from the cost estimate any loss in value because of depreciation; and (3) adds the value of the site alone to the depreciated cost figure.

The formula for the cost approach is:

$$\begin{array}{c}\text{Reproduction or}\\\text{Replacement}\\\text{Cost of Improvement(s)}\end{array} - \begin{array}{c}\text{Accrued}\\\text{Depreciation}\end{array} + \text{Site Value} = \begin{array}{c}\text{Property}\\\text{Value}\end{array}$$

The value of the land must be figured separately and then added to the depreciated construction cost of the structures. Site value typically is computed by the sales comparison approach, which was explained in the previous chapter. The location and improvements (exclusive of buildings) of the subject site are analyzed. The appraiser finds nearby recently sold properties that are comparable to the subject. Adjustments are made to the sales price of each of those properties to account for any significant differences between the comparable and the subject. The appraiser makes an estimate of the site value based on the adjusted values of the comparables.

Because the cost approach involves the addition of separately derived building and land values, it also is called the **summation method** of appraising.

121

THE THEORY BEHIND THE COST APPROACH

The basic premise of the cost approach is simple. Under normal market conditions, buyers of real estate typically do not want to pay more for a parcel with an existing structure than they would have to pay to build an identical structure on a vacant parcel. In the same manner, they would not want to pay as much for an older building as they would pay for a brand-new one. Every "used" building will have suffered some of the effects of ordinary wear and tear and may not be of the currently most desirable design or contain the most up-to-date fixtures. As a result, an older building should not be as expensive as a brand-new building of the same size that offers the features that are currently in the greatest demand.

There are exceptions to every rule, of course, and you may have already thought of several exceptions to the application of the cost approach to appraising real estate. Some properties are more valuable *because* of their age and are priced accordingly. Most urban areas have an historic district in which the historical landmark designation can be either a blessing or a bane. It can be a blessing if it means that property will retain its character and charm for the enjoyment of all who live in the community. It can be a bane for the property owner if considerable effort and financial commitment are required to bring the property to livable standards within the limitations typically placed on historic properties. Fortunately, our tax laws offer incentives to those who choose to invest in rehabilitating historic structures. Partly because of that advantage, habitable buildings with historic status tend to be more valuable than similar buildings without such a designation.

The realities of the marketplace also may appear to make a mockery of the cost approach. Most regions of the United States, at one time or another, have experienced the red-hot seller's market—the kind of market in which the typical property elicits multiple bids soon after being offered for sale. When an overabundance of buyers confronts a market with relatively few properties for sale, prices tend to rise at sometimes incomprehensible rates. Often, the cost of a "used" house rises to meet or even surpass that of a new house that may be less accessible or may not be immediately available for occupancy.

Most areas of the country have experienced the effects of a real estate boom at one time or another. Property owners in the Boston area in the mid-1980s, as well as those in Laughlin, Nevada, many parts of California and other cities throughout the country, can attest to the marvelous ease with which property can be sold in the seller's market that accompanies a real estate boom.

Unfortunately for sellers, but fortunately for buyers, most markets tend to cool off eventually. The tremendous rise in property values experienced by homeowners in Seattle and other cities in the Northwest in the late 1980s already had begun to taper off in 1990. Sometimes the cooling off is so precipitous that the boom turns into a bust and produces the opposite effect—the buyer's market. Many homeowners in the Boston area who had gleefully anticipated their potential profits during the hot days of the seller's market of the mid-1980s know the cold feeling of desperation that comes from having to sell a house that no one is interested in buying. Even worse, some of those who were buyers when prices reached all-time highs have been forced to sell their properties at a loss, the ultimate market dilemma that most of us don't like to think of in relation to our most valuable financial asset—our homes.

APPLYING THE COST APPROACH FORMULA

Several other, more technical drawbacks to the application of the cost approach exist, particularly when it is applied to residential property.

First, the existing property use may not be the land's highest and best use. If the structure being appraised is inappropriate, and not easily adaptable to the site's highest and best use, a cost approach analysis may be an idle exercise. One example that occurs frequently in urban areas is the residential neighborhood that is rezoned to allow commercial development. As properties in the area are converted to commercial use, their land value typically increases. The value of any structures may increase as well, but the structures with the greatest increase in value will be those that are adaptable for business use.

Second, builders' costs always vary to some extent, depending on the number of projects undertaken and the individual builder's profit margin, among other factors. The real estate appraiser's job is to be aware of the range of construction costs in the area in order to select the figure that is most appropriate for the property being appraised.

REPRODUCTION COST VERSUS REPLACEMENT COST

The appraiser always begins the cost approach valuation by estimating the construction cost of a new building that is physically or functionally identical to the building that is the subject of the appraisal, *at current prices*. The physical condition of the building and the outside factors that may affect its value are not considered at this stage. The construction cost computed by the appraiser will be either the reproduction or replacement cost of the subject. Although the terms *reproduction cost* and *replacement cost* may appear synonymous, they have very different meanings in a real estate appraisal.

Reproduction Cost

Reproduction cost is the dollar amount required to produce an exact duplicate of a building at current prices. The appraiser must take into account the expense of finding materials of the same design, manufacture and quality as the subject property, constructed with the same techniques.

For properties that were constructed in the post–World War II era, this is usually a feasible task that results in a cost analysis in keeping with other structures of current vintage. For older buildings, however, particularly those that have attained "historic" status, the task of estimating the current reproduction cost becomes considerably more formidable. The appraiser is confronted with materials that may no longer be available or that may be impossible to duplicate except at an exorbitant cost. In addition, certain property features requiring sophisticated carpentry, masonry or other skills may be beyond the expertise of today's craftspeople.

Because most existing structures are fairly recent in origin, finding the reproduction cost usually is not a problem and is how appraisers use the cost approach. For properties that do not have an economically viable reproduction cost, the appraiser instead will calculate the replacement cost of the structures.

Replacement Cost

Replacement cost is the current construction cost of a building with the same **utility** as the subject structure. The appraiser actually is estimating the reproduction cost, but it is the reproduction cost of a theoretical building that contains the same number, type and size of rooms as the building being appraised and that can be used in the same way. The appraiser does not take into account the many details of material and workmanship that may make the subject property unique. The theoretical building against which the subject is measured should possess the same overall quality as the subject, but as defined by contemporary standards.

Of course, the appraiser will note as a condition of the appraisal that it is impossible to duplicate the subject property exactly in today's marketplace. The appraiser also will have to gauge the effect of this condition on the property's value. The existing property features may be more or less valuable, depending on the desirability of those features in the marketplace.

For example, an older home may have intricate exterior and interior carpentry well beyond the type of work available today. In such a case, the appraiser will estimate the cost to produce features of a similar quality, using currently available construction materials and methods. Many architectural details, such as elaborate moldings (ceiling trim), can be found in materials that look identical to the originals from which they are copied. Yet, because the copies are formed from lightweight, synthetic materials, they are relatively inexpensive and easy to install. Figure 8.1 shows some of the types of trim pieces, for exterior or interior use, that can be formed from polyurethane.

FIGURE 8.1   Ornamental Finishing Materials

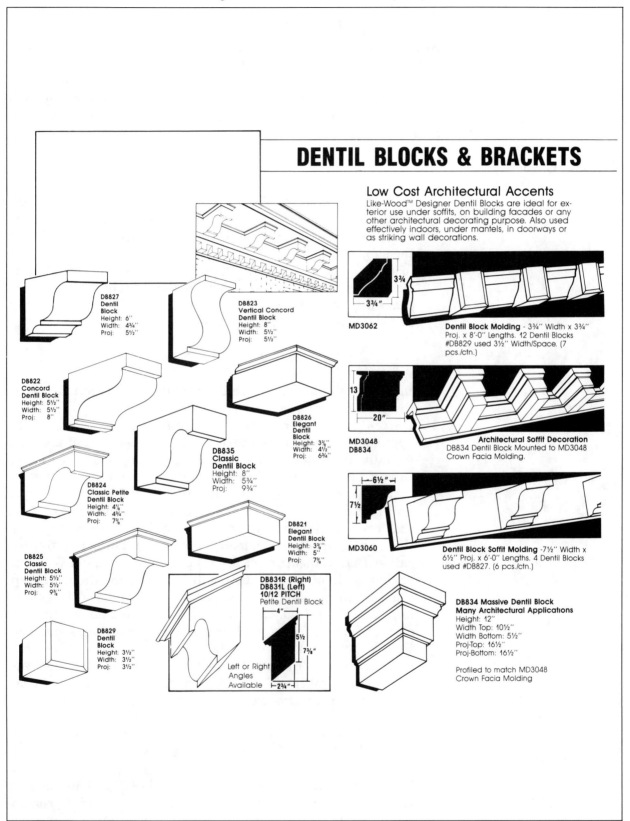

DENTIL BLOCKS & BRACKETS

Low Cost Architectural Accents
Like-Wood™ Designer Dentil Blocks are ideal for exterior use under soffits, on building facades or any other architectural decorating purpose. Also used effectively indoors, under mantels, in doorways or as striking wall decorations.

MD3062

Dentil Block Molding - 3¾" Width x 3¾" Proj. x 8'-0" Lengths. 12 Dentil Blocks #DB829 used 3½" Width/Space. (7 pcs./ctn.)

MD3048
DB834

Architectural Soffit Decoration
DB834 Dentil Block Mounted to MD3048 Crown Facia Molding.

MD3060

Dentil Block Soffit Molding -7½" Width x 6½" Proj. x 6'-0" Lengths. 4 Dentil Blocks used #DB827. (6 pcs./ctn.)

DB834 Massive Dentil Block
Many Architectural Applications
Height: 12"
Width Top: 10½"
Width Bottom: 5½"
Proj-Top: 16½"
Proj-Bottom: 16½"

Profiled to match MD3048
Crown Facia Molding

DB827
Dentil Block
Height: 6"
Width: 4¾"
Proj: 5½"

DB823
Vertical Concord Dentil Block
Height: 8"
Width: 5½"
Proj: 5½"

DB822
Concord Dentil Block
Height: 5½"
Width: 5½"
Proj: 8"

DB826
Elegant Dentil Block
Height: 3¾"
Width: 4½"
Proj: 6¾"

DB835
Classic Dentil Block
Height: 8"
Width: 5¾"
Proj: 9¾"

DB824
Classic Petite Dentil Block
Height: 4⅛"
Width: 4¾"
Proj: 7⅜"

DB821
Elegant Dentil Block
Height: 3¾"
Width: 5"
Proj: 7⅞"

DB825
Classic Dentil Block
Height: 5½"
Width: 5½"
Proj: 9⅞"

DB829
Dentil Block
Height: 3½"
Width: 3½"
Proj: 3½"

DB834R (Right)
DB831L (Left)
10/12 PITCH
Petite Dentil Block

Left or Right
Angles
Available

Source: Like-Wood™, 2550 Boyce Plaza Road, Pittsburgh, PA 15241.

FINDING THE REPRODUCTION COST

Four basic methods can be used to find the building reproduction cost. The most complex are used primarily for commercial and industrial properties. The first method described—the square-foot method—is the one that is used most often when appraising single-family residences. The other methods of computing construction cost are described to give you some idea of how other structures are appraised.

Methods Used

1. *Square foot method.* With the **square foot method,** the current construction cost per square foot of the type of building being appraised is multiplied by the number of square feet in the subject property. For example, the current cost per square foot of a single-story warehouse storage facility in the Rolling Hills area is about $65. Because the warehouse being appraised is 45,000 square feet, its estimated construction cost at today's prices can be computed:

$$45,000 \times \$65 = \$2,925,000$$

In this example, the current estimated construction cost of the property being appraised is $2,925,000.

2. *Unit-in-place method.* Using the **unit-in-place method,** the appraiser computes the construction cost per unit of measure (usually, price per square foot) of each component part of the subject building, including the dollar amounts necessary for material, labor, overhead and builder's profit. The cost per unit of measure then is multiplied by the number of units of that component part in the subject building. In some cases, the unit is a single element, such as a plumbing fixture, rather than a measure of area. For example, one of the component parts of the building will be the foundation. The appraiser will measure the cost per measured unit of the type of foundation required. In this example, the foundation consists of a 12-inch concrete wall and footings covering a building that is 100 by 125 feet. The current cost to build such a foundation is $30.70 per linear foot. The appraiser first estimates the number of linear feet in the foundation, then computes the construction cost of that building component:

$$100' + 100' + 125' + 125' = 450 \text{ linear feet}$$
$$450 \times \$30.70 = \$13,815$$

The current cost of the foundation is $13,815. This amount will be added to the cost of each of the other building components, such as floor, framing, roof construction, windows, doors, and heating, air-conditioning and plumbing fixtures, to derive the total current construction cost of the building being appraised.

3. *Quantity survey method.* In the **quantity survey method,** direct and indirect construction costs are itemized separately, then totaled. Direct construction costs are those related to materials and labor, such as clearing the land, laying the foundation, lumber and carpentry, drywall and installation, cabinetry, electrical wiring, plumbing and fixtures. Indirect costs include such expenses as building permit, overhead, payroll taxes and builder's profit. For example, an eight-unit apartment building could be constructed today at a cost of $630,383 for all materials and labor. Indirect construction costs, including building permit, survey, layout, payroll taxes, insurance, builder's overhead and profit, would be $75,050. When appraising the building, the direct and indirect costs would be totaled:

$$\$630,383 + \$75,050 = \$705,433$$

The building's current construction cost is $705,433.

4. *Index method.* With the **index method,** the appraiser applies a factor representing the change in building costs over time to the original cost of the subject property. For example, consider a building that originally cost $100,000 to build in 1973. The cost index factor for 1973 is 100, while the cost index factor for the present year is 378. The current construction cost of the subject building can be computed:

$$\$100,000 \times {}^{378}\!/_{100} =$$
$$\$100,000 \times 3.78 =$$
$$\$378,000$$

In this example, the current estimated reproduction cost of the subject structure is $378,000. Because this method of estimating reproduction cost fails to take into account the many variables that can affect construction costs, it never should be used as the sole method of determining the construction cost, but only as a quick means of double-checking the estimate reached by one of the other methods.

Applying the Square Foot Method

With experience, the appraiser can become as familiar with local building costs as a contractor is. One of the ways in which both building and appraisal professionals keep up to date on current costs is by using a **cost manual.** Information on building specifications and typical construction costs is provided in manuals published by such national companies as Boeckh Publications, F. W. Dodge Corporation, Marshall and Swift Publication Company and R. S. Means Company. Cost manuals are customized for

FIGURE 8.2   Typical Page from a Residential Cost Manual

Average 2 Story		Living Area	2000 S.F.
		Perimeter	135 L.F.

		MAN-HOURS	COST PER SQUARE FOOT OF LIVING AREA		
			MAT.	LABOR	TOTAL
1 Site Work	Site preparation for slab; trench 4' deep for foundation wall.	.034		.67	.67
2 Foundations	Continuous concrete footing 8" deep x 18" wide; cast-in-place concrete wall, 8" thick, 4' deep, 4" concrete slab on 4" crushed stone base, trowel finish.	.066	1.77	1.87	3.64
3 Framing	2" x 4" wood studs, 16" O.C.; 1/2" plywood sheathing; 2" x 6" rafters 16" O.C. with 1/2" plywood sheathing, 4 in 12 pitch; 2" x 6" ceiling joists 16" O.C.; 2" x 8" floor joists 16" O.C. with bridging and 5/8" waferboard subfloor; 1/2" waferboard subfloor on 1" x 2" wood sleepers 16" O.C.	.131	3.62	4.15	7.77
4 Exterior Walls	Horizontal beveled wood siding; #15 felt building paper; 3-1/2" batt insulation; wood double hung windows; 3 flush solid core wood exterior doors; storms and screens.	.111	8.71	3.76	12.47
5 Roofing	240# asphalt shingles; #15 felt building paper; aluminum flashing; 6" attic insulation. Aluminum gutters and downspouts.	.024	.39	.59	.98
6 Interiors	1/2" drywall, taped and finished, painted with primer and 1 coat; softwood baseboard and trim, painted with primer and 1 coat; finished hardwood floor 40%, carpet with underlayment 40%, vinyl tile with underlayment 15%, ceramic tile with underlayment 5%; hollow core doors.	.232	9.28	7.90	17.18
7 Specialties	Kitchen cabinets - 14 L.F. wall and base cabinets with laminated plastic counter top; medicine cabinet, stairs.	.021	.93	.33	1.26
8 Mechanical	1 lavatory, white, wall hung; 1 water closet, white; 1 bathtub with shower, porcelain enamel steel, white; 1 kitchen sink, stainless steel, single; 1 water heater, gas fired, 30 gal.; gas fired forced air heat.	.060	1.57	1.34	2.91
9 Electrical	200 Amp. service; romex wiring; incandescent lighting fixtures, switches, receptacles.	.039	.50	.80	1.30
10 Overhead	Contractor's overhead and profit.		1.87	1.50	3.37
Total			28.64	22.91	51.55

Source: *Means Residential Cost Data 1991 Edition,* p. 29. R.S. Means Company, Inc., Construction Consultants & Publishers, Kingston, Mass.

specific geographic regions and usually are updated at least annually and sometimes even monthly. The newest approach is to use a computerized data base that can be accessed via telephone modem to a terminal screen in the customer's office. A page from a typical residential cost manual appears in Figure 8.2.

The cost manual illustrated in Figure 8.2 uses both qualitative and quantitative cost breakdowns. The building is first categorized by the quality of its construction, in ascending order: economy, average, custom or luxury. Next, the typical cost per square foot is broken down into basic building components, from site work to overhead. In this way, the cost estimate for the subject property can be further individualized.

In addition to this very broad itemization of building costs, the manual also lists separate construction features, such as window systems, in a separate section in greater detail and gives cost figures for both materials and labor. Finally, tables provide multiplication factors that take into account the regional variances in material, labor and other costs. For example, a factor of 1.21 for San Francisco, California, indicates that a home in San Francisco typically will cost 21 percent more than the standard used in the manual.

Most libraries will provide copies of construction cost manuals. Many newspapers also publish periodic listings of average home-construction costs in the area.

EXAMPLE:

Josephine and Martin Smith own a two-story home in Leafy Meadow, North Carolina. The house, which is 15 years old, is of average quality construction for the area and has a total of 2,000 square feet. A current cost manual available at the public library suggests that typical construction costs for a two-story home of the same quality and with the same features are $55 per square foot. The manual also lists a regional factor of .85 for Leafy Meadow, North Carolina. This differential takes into account the relatively low costs of labor and certain materials in Leafy Meadow. The total cost and regional influence can be computed:

$$2,000 \times \$55 = \$110,000$$
$$\$110,000 \times .85 = \$93,500$$

Using the cost-manual information, the current cost to build the Smith house is estimated as $93,500.

ACCRUED DEPRECIATION

Depreciation is the kind of term that everyone can define, yet few people can apply. **Depreciation** is a loss in value from *any* cause.

Accrued depreciation is the total loss in value from all causes as of the date of the appraisal. There are three basic forms of depreciation:

1. **Physical deterioration** is the actual destruction of a building, whether from natural or human-made forces. Physical deterioration can occur gradually, as when a building undergoes ordinary wear and tear. It also can happen quickly, for example, when a building is damaged by occupants (rock through a window) or by natural forces (a storm or earthquake).

2. **Functional obsolescence** takes place when a building's layout, design or other features are considered undesirable in comparison with features designed for the same functions in newer properties. In new homes with two or more bedrooms, one bedroom typically is designated as the "master bedroom" and is sized accordingly. If the home has three or more bedrooms, it almost always will have more than one bathroom, and one of the bathrooms will adjoin the master bedroom. The three-bedroom home that does not have a master suite, or which has only one bathroom, may be functionally obsolete, depending on what buyers in the area expect.

3. **External obsolescence** is loss in value from any cause outside the subject property. External obsolescence also is called **environmental, economic** or **locational** obsolescence. These synonyms give you some idea of the range of the outside factors that can lower property values. The most conspicuous source of external obsolescence these days may be the environmental hazard. Proximity to a known hazard, even when the subject property can be scientifically demonstrated to be unaffected directly by the hazard, will tend to lower property value.

Some form of depreciation, at least physical deterioration, begins the moment a building is completed. The building will suffer some type of depreciation during its entire **economic life,** the period during which it can be used for its originally intended purpose. A building's economic life also is called its **useful life.** Economic life is not necessarily the length of time that the building is expected to remain standing, which is its **physical life.** Of course, not all buildings deteriorate as rapidly as others, and some will benefit from better upkeep. If a building has received regular maintenance and repair, its **effective age** (apparent age) may be less than its actual age.

For appraisal purposes, the most important time measure is the building's **remaining economic life.** This is the period from the date of the appraisal during which the building can be expected to remain useful for its original purpose.

Although the definition of depreciation is simple enough, it can be confusing to understand and difficult to compute. One source of confusion stems from the fact that the property also is depreciated for tax purposes. Depreciation for tax purposes has no relationship to the depreciation that an appraiser will measure to determine property value. Tax depreciation is a means of writing off (deducting from income) the cost of a building over whatever term of years is permitted by law. Because the federal government recognizes that a building is a deteriorating asset, it allows the cost of the building to be balanced against income produced by it, in yearly increments. The term over which the depreciation is taken, however, has no relationship to either the age or the condition of the property. In fact, both the term of years and the rate of depreciation per year are factors the Internal Revenue Service (IRS) changes often at the will of Congress.

The computations for tax depreciation are involved more with the impact of the allowed deduction on current tax income than with the extent to which the property has deteriorated or otherwise suffered a loss in value. Generally, taxpayers are happier when depreciation deductions are allowed over fewer years (creating a higher deduction per year) and tax collectors are happier when depreciation deductions are spread out over a longer term. Throughout the rest of this chapter and book, therefore, depreciation will refer to a property's actual loss in value and not the arbitrary rate of loss dictated by the tax laws.

Appraisers use several methods to measure depreciation. They are as follows.

Economic Age-Life Method

The **economic age-life method** of computing depreciation is the simplest to understand and use. The building's construction cost is divided by the number of years of its economic life to find a yearly dollar amount of depreciation. The yearly amount of depreciation then is multiplied by the effective age of the building to determine the total amount by which it has depreciated. As a formula, the economic age-life method is:

$$\frac{\text{Building Cost}}{\text{Number of Years of Economic Life}} \times \text{Effective Age} = \frac{\text{Total Accrued}}{\text{Depreciation}}$$

Figure 8.3 shows how the relationship between building cost and projected age can be graphed along a straight line. For this reason, the economic age-life method also is called the **straight-line** method of computing depreciation. The remaining building value at any building age can be found by finding the point on the graphed line where the age factor intersects the cost factor.

In the example plotted in Figure 8.3, the current building cost is $200,000 and the estimated economic life of the building is 50 years. When the building has an economic life of 40 years, its remaining value will be $40,000 because it will have depreciated by $160,000.

FIGURE 8.3   Economic Age-Life Depreciation

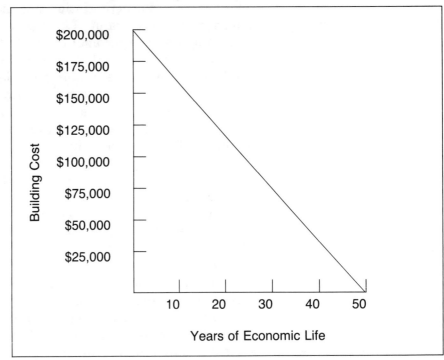

The economic age-life method of computing depreciation fails to take into account the many variables that can cause a loss in value. For this reason, its use requires that the amount and kinds of depreciation the property has undergone be fairly straightforward (generally, ordinary wear and tear) and also typical of the area. Because most properties will require a more detailed depreciation analysis, another method may have to be used, at least for certain items.

Observed-Condition Method

In the **observed-condition method** of computing depreciation, the appraiser analyzes the property in terms of each of the separate categories of depreciation. The appraiser notes whether each item of depreciation is *curable,* if it can be easily and economically repaired or replaced, or *incurable,* if repairs would be cumbersome or too expensive. This method also is called the **breakdown method**.

Curable physical deterioration includes such repairs as a broken appliance or window and other items of routine maintenance. Examples of **incurable physical deterioration** include those building components that could be repaired or replaced only with great difficulty, such as a foundation that has suffered mudslide damage. Ordinarily, these building components are expected to last for the life of the building. Loss caused by physical deterioration can be valued as a percentage of total building value, or the appraiser can value each depreciated item separately.

Functional obsolescence includes physical or design features that are inadequate or undesirable by current standards. Functional obsolescence can be **curable** if the existing layout or design can be changed economically. For example, a bedroom next to the kitchen could be converted to a desired family room or den. Most often, however, functional obsolescence is **incurable.** A typical example is the room layout that could be changed only by expensive remodeling, such as a bedroom that can be entered solely through another bedroom.

Another common example of functional obsolescence is the outdated kitchen. If a property seller is willing to modernize appliances and cabinets, the amount spent remodeling the outdated kitchen may result in an equal increase in value, depending on market demand. The loss in value for appraisal purposes is calculated as the amount by which the entire property value could be increased by making the improvement, rather than the improvement's actual cost to the property owner. In other words, not every dollar spent will result in a corresponding dollar increase in value. This is an important point to remember if a homeowner is considering a remodeling project solely as a means of making the home more salable.

External obsolescence is considered **incurable** only. Because this form of depreciation is caused by factors outside the property, the owner most likely has no immediate, practical way of remedying it. The interstate highway that creates noise and pollution for nearby residents may be an annoying fact of life, but a fact of life, nonetheless. Don't forget that external obsolescence can be caused by economic factors. The appraiser should be acutely aware of the effect on value of a depressed real estate market. In particular, the appraiser should note the apparent effect of economic conditions on recent sales or rentals of comparable properties.

Sales Comparison Method

With the **sales comparison method** of computing depreciation, the appraiser uses the sales prices of comparable properties to derive the value of a depreciated feature. By analyzing enough comparable properties, the appraiser isolates the value of the depreciated feature. This method also is referred to as the **market comparison method.**

ITEMIZING ACCRUED DEPRECIATION

Total accrued depreciation is calculated by listing each of the categories of depreciation, estimating the loss in value attributable to each of the categories and totaling the amounts listed.

EXAMPLE:

The Firestone house is being appraised. After conducting a thorough examination of the property, the appraiser estimates the following items of curable physical depreciation:

Item	Reproduction Cost	Percent Depreciation	Amount of Depreciation
Carpeting	$3,500	20%	$700
Air-Conditioner Compressor	1,400	70%	980
Water Heater	350	100%	350

The total reproduction cost of the depreciated items is $3,500 + $1,400 + $350, or $5,250. The total amount of depreciation represented by those items is $700 + $980 + $350, or $2,030.

Because other forms of physical deterioration generally are based on overall wear and tear, the appraiser will determine a percentage of depreciation for all remaining items and apply that percentage, *after* subtracting the reproduction cost of the items separately depreciated.

General wear and tear to the Firestone house is estimated at 20 percent of its $130,000 reproduction cost. Depreciation caused by physical deterioration is thus estimated:

$$\$130,000 - \$5,250 = \$124,750$$
$$\$124,750 \times 20\% = \$24,950$$
$$\$24,950 + \$2,030 = \$26,980$$

The appraiser will note $26,980 as a deduction from the construction cost for physical deterioration. The next category of depreciation is functional obsolescence.

The Firestone house has three bedrooms and off the master bedroom is a separate room, which can be entered only from the master bedroom. The "extra" room serves as a home office and den. This arrangement actually was a building option offered by the developer. Instead of leaving a wall opening in this room for a doorway from the hall, the builder placed the only entrance in a wall shared with the master bedroom. Very few homes in the subdivision utilize this option. Most homes have four bedrooms, all with separate entrances. In this area, prospective buyers typically want four bedrooms and are likely to want to use this space for a bedroom, which means that any other arrangement is awkward and undesirable. The appraiser considers this a form of functional obsolescence. By analyzing sales of other properties in the area with similar features, the appraiser determines that the fact that this fourth "bedroom" does not have a separate entrance indicates that the market value of the house is approximately $3,000 less.

The deduction from the reproduction cost for functional obsolescence is $3,000. The final category of depreciation is external obsolescence.

The Firestone house is located in a quiet residential neighborhood that originally was developed about 20 years ago. The zoning is entirely single-family residential, houses generally have been well maintained and the close proximity of the area to the suburban business district has resulted in a steady market demand. There are no nearby nuisances and no foreseeable changes to the surrounding land uses. As a result, the appraiser determines that no adjustment is necessary for external obsolescence.

Deductions for depreciation are $26,980 for physical deterioration and $3,000 for functional obsolescence, making the total accrued depreciation $29,980. Land value already has been estimated at $35,000. The appraiser is ready to compute a market value estimate by the cost approach:

Reproduction Cost	$130,000
Less Accrued Depreciation	– 29,980
Subtotal	$100,020
Plus Land Value	35,000
Estimated Market Value	$135,020

The estimated market value of the Firestone house using the cost approach is $135,020.

USEFULNESS OF THE COST APPROACH

The reproduction cost of a building tends to set the upper limit of its value. There can be a significant difference between the current cost to reproduce a structure and its market value, however. If the improvements are not new, the appraiser must estimate the amount of accrued depreciation that the property has suffered and deduct that amount from the reproduction cost. For very old buildings, estimating depreciation will be much more difficult. Added to that problem is the fact that today's marketplace may not produce any suitable equivalents to the construction materials and techniques used in an older structure. For those buildings, the sales comparison or income capitalization approaches may be most appropriate.

The cost approach is especially useful when valuing buildings for which the sales comparison approach or income capitalization approach is impracticable. Examples include schools, museums, libraries and other institutional structures. Generally, few, if any, comparable sales for such properties will exist, and no income figures will be available.

For certain appraisal purposes, the cost approach may be the *only* feasible approach. In an appraisal for insurance purposes, for instance, insured value will be based on the cost of restoration, which will dictate the amount of reimbursement for loss.

EXAMPLE: A Tale of Two Houses

The Newsomes and the Palermos own houses on Oak Street in the town of Riverdale, Ohio. Both families purchased their homes when the subdivision was first developed ten years ago.

The Palermos have maintained their home with meticulous attention. Even the garage, with its shelving designed by Mrs. Palermo and built by Mr. Palermo, is spotless. The Palermos simply enjoy all forms of household chores. They recently devoted a week of vacation time to repainting the exterior of their house in a soft colonial blue.

The Newsomes, on the other hand, hate working around the house almost as much as they hate paying someone else to do so. As a result, their home, though only a block away and of the same age, design and construction quality as the Palermos' house, has developed some obvious, as well as some not-so-obvious, problems.

The exterior and interior of the Newsome house have an overall tired appearance. There are numerous marks on the walls and the rugs. The grease-stained kitchen cabinets and appliances bear the scars of many careless gestures. The mantel above the fireplace has been darkened by smoke. The ceramic tile in the shower stalls is broken in some places and discolored from years of grime, mold and mildew that never has been adequately removed. In one of the bedrooms, the walls have been severely battered by an overzealous child learning to tap dance. The tile on the laundry floor is buckling because the washing machine discharge hose continually leaks.

The Newsomes' garage door can't be lifted ever since one of the hinges pulled out of the frame when someone accidentally drove into it. The Newsomes don't mind, for they prefer to use their garage for storing their collection of broken appliances, rather than for parking. Outside, things aren't any better. The paint on the wood siding is peeling badly. The rain gutters never have been cleaned, and one section of gutter is dangling since it collapsed from the weight of accumulated debris and ice during the past winter. Last but not least, the shrubbery is unkempt and the lawn has been taken over by weeds.

Pamela Palermo and Frank Newsome work for the same company, which has announced that it is relocating to a smaller city about 325 miles from Riverdale. Pamela and Frank both are invited to make the move. The company will pay for their moving expenses and will reimburse them for their home sale expenses, as well, including the brokerage commission. The Palermos and the Newsomes decide to take the company up on its offer. Both families call on the same real estate agent for a market analysis of the sales potential of their homes.

The Palermos are pleased when the agent compliments them on the beautiful appearance of their yard and home. As they relax around the dining room table, the agent tells them that, based on sales of similar properties in the neighborhood, the market value of their home should fall in the range of $160,000 to $170,000. The Palermos then talk with several other agents, who make a similar value analysis.

Down the street, the Newsomes are anxious to hear what the agent has to say about the value of their home. The agent is very pleasant as she walks around and through the house, even though she trips on the edge of the tile floor in the laundry room and narrowly avoids walking into the dangling gutter. Because the Newsomes know that the Palermos have just listed their property with the same agent for $165,000, they expect that she will suggest a similar figure for their house. They are very surprised, however, when the agent tells them that she strongly recommends that they have a structural pest-control inspection to confirm or eliminate the possibility of termite damage. Apart from any work indicated by the termite report, she believes that the market value of their home is somewhere in the range of $150,000 to $160,000, *if* they clean and paint the entire house, inside and out, replace the laundry room tile floor, clean out the garage, fix the broken garage door, repair the damaged bedroom walls, retile the bathrooms and repair or replace the gutters. The yard area should be reseeded or at least weeded and the shrubbery pruned. They also should consider refinishing the kitchen cabinets. If they don't accomplish these tasks, their house probably is worth considerably less than $150,000 and, if they're serious about selling, they shouldn't ask more than $140,000 to $145,000 for it to attract a buyer. The agent's explanation refers to such things as "deferred maintenance," "deterioration" and "curb appeal."

The Newsomes, when they recover from their shock, decide to contact a few other agents. Unfortunately, the value estimates don't seem to get any higher. Frank Newsome schedules a meeting with his company's relocation officer to find out whether the company will pay for the necessary maintenance and repairs to his home as "expenses of sale." He isn't reassured by the answer he receives, but he decides to go ahead with the job transfer and home sale despite what he calls the "lousy" real estate market.

The Newsomes shouldn't have been surprised at the low valuation of their home in comparison to that of the Palermos. Even though the homes are in the same neighborhood and are comparable in size, design and quality of construction, the Palermos have maintained their home diligently over the years, while the Newsomes have neglected theirs. The results of these efforts (or lack thereof) show in the general condition and appearance of the two homes.

APPRAISAL WORKSHEET

1. When was the subject house built? _____

2. How old is it now? _____

3. How old are other buildings in the neighborhood? _____

4. What is the cost per square foot of similar new houses? _____

5. Are the materials and construction techniques used to build the subject house in common use today? _____

6. Does the neighborhood have other houses with design and construction features comparable to those of the subject house? _____

7. What unique design or construction features does the house have? _____
    _____

8. What design or construction feature does the house have that are considered undesirable by today's homebuyers? _____

9. What is the zoning for the neighborhood and is it expected to change in the future?
    _____

10. Are nearby land uses compatible with the neighborhood? _____

11. What adverse environmental influences are there in the neighborhood and what has been their impact on property values? _____

12. How can economic conditions (the current market) be expected to affect the value of the house? _____
    _____

Rate each of the following features of the property as good, average, fair or poor:

	Good	Average	Fair	Poor
General exterior condition	____	____	____	____
Exterior siding	____	____	____	____
Masonry	____	____	____	____
Gutters and trim	____	____	____	____
General interior condition	____	____	____	____
Floors	____	____	____	____
Walls and ceilings	____	____	____	____
Cabinets and wood trim	____	____	____	____
Bathrooms	____	____	____	____
Fixtures (heating unit, water heater, appliances)	____	____	____	____
Garage condition	____	____	____	____
Landscaping				
Design	____	____	____	____
Upkeep	____	____	____	____
Amenities (porch, deck, pool)	____	____	____	____

9

The Income Capitalization Approach

Although the income capitalization approach has a formidable title, it is based on a relatively simple premise: The value of a property is related to the income it can produce. The more income the property produces, the more the property tends to be worth. An investor will pay more for a property that produces a certain level of income than for a property that produces less income.

The income capitalization approach is most useful, of course, for properties that are purchased strictly for their ability to produce income. These typically include commercial properties, such as office buildings and retail stores. Less often, investors purchase industrial properties, such as manufacturing plants, for their income potential. An investor determines the price to offer for a potential acquisition by studying the income generated by the property and by determining the present value of the right to receive that income in the future, taking into account the rate of income, or capitalization rate, that the investor expects to receive.

The formula for the **income capitalization approach** is:

$$\frac{\text{Net Operating Income}}{\text{Capitalization Rate}} = \text{Value}$$

The income capitalization approach usually is the most appropriate appraisal method to use for commercial properties, which generally are purchased for their income-producing potential. The same can be said of residential property with more than four dwelling units. The buyer of an apartment building will be interested in the cash flow the property generates, that is, the amount of profit that can be expected over and above the expenses of ownership. Smaller multiunit buildings with only two to four apartments also can be purchased primarily for their income-producing potential, but very often they are owner-occupied, and the benefits of living in the building have to be weighed against the loss of income from the owner-occupied unit.

Single-family houses, on the other hand, usually are not purchased for their income-producing potential. Even though many single-family homes are purchased by investors, the vast majority of single-family residences are owner-occupied, and the amount of income they could generate is not a factor in the decision to buy. Still, a variation of the income capitalization approach can be used by anyone who is interested in the income-producing capability of a single-family house. This approach compares the monthly rent paid for similar homes to the sales prices of those homes to derive a factor that can be multiplied by the income expected from the subject property to calculate market value. The formula for the **gross income multiplier method** is:

$$\text{Potential Gross Income} \times \text{Gross Income Multiplier} = \text{Value}$$

This chapter will cover the types of information required to apply either version of the income capitalization approach, as well as the ways in which the information is derived.

DETERMINING INCOME

Because the income capitalization approach is concerned with the amount of income a piece of real estate produces, the first data to be collected by the appraiser using this method will be complete information on the potential gross income the property can generate. The appraiser will take into account both rental income and income from other sources, such as vending machines, parking fees, etc. Even the term *rent* takes into account several different possible figures, as you will read next.

Rents

Even though a building may be fully occupied by reliable, long-term tenants, the appraiser must consider not only the present rents paid, but also past rents as well as rents currently paid for comparable properties in the area.

Rent currently being paid by agreement between tenant and landlord is called **scheduled rent** or **contract rent.** For income properties such as stores, offices and warehouses, scheduled rent usually is stated as the rent per square foot per year. The usual practice in stating apartment rents is to quote the scheduled rent per unit per year, which then is broken down to the rent per room per year. The appraiser's data on scheduled rent usually comes from the lessee (the tenant, the person renting the property), the lessor (the landlord, the owner of the property) or the real estate agent who manages the property or who may have handled a recent sale.

Market rent is the appraiser's estimate of a property's rent *potential*. Market rent is the rent the property can be expected to command in the current market, considering what tenants have paid and are paying for the subject property and other, comparable properties. Market rent is not necessarily the rent paid by current tenants.

The appraiser also will be interested in **historical rent,** which is the rent paid in past years. Historical rent data for both the subject and similar properties will tell the appraiser whether the market appears to be following a trend, and whether current rent information is likely to be reliable. Again, the appraiser can acquire the needed data from the tenant, landlord or real estate broker or perhaps from the appraiser's own files.

Other Income

Rents may not be the only source of income. Even a small apartment building may provide coin-operated laundry machines, an amenity that appeals to tenants. Office buildings may offer food and other vending machines, and in larger buildings, the lessor may operate a newspaper stand or convenience store on the premises. A parking area may provide substantial additional income. Any income received must be taken into consideration, for it will be a factor in determining market value.

In making up a statement of potential gross income, the appraiser will list rent and nonrent income separately, then total them. Because the appraiser is itemizing *potential* gross income, the total very likely will be somewhat higher than the actual rent income received for the current year. At this point, for instance, the appraiser totals the expected rent income from all rental units, even though some units may be vacant and some tenants may be in arrears in payment of rent. The appraiser also must include in the potential gross income calculation the rental value of any owner-occupied areas or caretaker's quarters. The value of the use of these areas, even if the current occupant does not pay rent, must be considered.

Income data received from the property owner always should be verified by the tenants, real estate broker or rental agent.

Effective Gross Income

At this point, the appraiser makes an adjustment to the potential gross income to allow for the fact that the rental units probably will not be fully occupied 100 percent of the time, and some tenants will be slow or fail to pay the scheduled rent. To derive **effective gross income,** the appraiser must estimate a reasonable percentage of income to represent **vacancy and collection**

losses that can be expected to occur over the course of a year, and subtract that amount from potential gross income. Factors to be taken into account include:

1. Present and past rental losses of the property;
2. Present and past rental levels for other properties in the area that are in competition with the subject property;
3. Area population and economic trends;
4. Reliability of tenants; and
5. Length of existing leases.

Under ordinary market conditions (neither boom nor bust), the allowance for vacancy and collection losses typically is in the five- to ten-percent range. If the area has experienced any amount of "overbuilding" or for whatever reason has much more property available than current market demand warrants, the vacancy factor may be considerably higher. If the area's economy is experiencing a recession or depression, collection losses as well as vacancies will tend to be higher than normal. On the other hand, if there is a heavier-than-normal demand for space relative to the number of available properties, the appraiser may determine that a lower allowance for vacancy and collection losses is indicated.

Net Operating Income

Having found the effective gross income, the appraiser can deduct the property's *operating expenses* to derive the **net operating income. Operating expenses** are those costs incurred to maintain the property and to continue the income stream. Such costs include employee salaries and benefits, utility payments, management fees, legal and accounting fees, insurance and real estate taxes. Other costs also are considered for appraisal purposes, but are not considered for accounting purposes, and vice versa. Operating expenses for appraisal purposes include **reserves for replacement,** the fund that is accumulated so that major expenditures for the replacement of building components can be made, but the payments themselves as they are made are not considered operating expenses for appraisal purposes.

Although they are an important part of the accountant's calculation, for appraisal purposes, operating expenses do *not* include the costs to the owner to finance the purchase. The appraiser also does not take into account building depreciation deductions, which may have substantial income tax impact for the property owner. The appraiser is interested in the property's value as an income producer apart from any effect its ownership may have on a particular investor's after-tax cash flow.

Reconstructing the Operating Statement

The appraiser's estimates and computations are summarized in an **operating statement** for the property being appraised. Because the appraiser's operating statement will include some important differences from the accountant's operating statement for the same property, this process is referred to as **reconstructing** the operating statement. Figure 9.1 is an example of a reconstructed operating statement that shows the accountant's figures as well as the appraiser's calculations.

For the example in Figure 9.1, the appraiser considered the past, present and expected future rental performance of an eight-unit apartment building. Present income was adjusted upward to reflect the rental value of an apartment occupied by the owner. Vacancy and collection losses, based on an area study, were estimated at five percent of the rental income. The owner uses the services of a part-time handyman and a part-time gardener. Roof replacement is expected every 20 years at a cost of $20,000, requiring a reserve fund of $1,000 per year. Plumbing and electri-

FIGURE 9.1   Operating Statement

	Accountant's Figures	Appraiser's Adjusted Estimate
Gross Income (Rent)	$87,000.00	$92,000
Allowance for Vacancies and Bad Debts	——	4,600
Effective Gross Income	——	87,400
Operating Expenses		
Salaries and wages	12,000.00	12,000
Employees' benefits	1,847.32	1,900
Electricity	1,464.50	1,500
Gas	4,323.00	4,300
Water	700.10	700
Painting and decorating	1,600.00	1,600
Supplies	938.79	900
Repairs	3,530.00	3,500
Management	5,000.00	5,000
Legal and accounting fees	1,500.00	1,500
Miscellaneous expenses	600.00	600
Insurance (three-year policy)	4,200.00	4,200
Real estate taxes	7,000.00	7,000
Reserves—		
Roof replacement	——	1,000
Plumbing and electrical	——	1,500
Payments on air conditioners	1,600.00	——
Principal on mortgage	1,800.00	——
Interest on mortgage	18,945.00	——
Depreciation—building	12,000.00	——
Total Expenses	$79,048.71	$47,200
Net Operating Income	$7,951.29	$40,200

cal replacements are based on a 20-year service life for fixtures costing $30,000, requiring a reserve fund of $1,500 per year. The appraiser will not include:

- Payments for capital improvements, such as air conditioners;
- Principal and mortgage interest payments, because the property is being appraised on a "free and clear" basis; or
- Depreciation, which is calculated by the accountant on the basis of the depreciation schedule allowed by the IRS for federal income tax purposes.

SELECTING THE CAPITALIZATION RATE

The average investor will expect an income-producing property to provide both a return *on* the investment (profit on the amount invested) and a return *of* the investment (the amount invested). The real estate investment shares the same basic rationale as any investment. The first investment most people make is to deposit cash in a bank account. The depositor expects to earn a certain rate of interest on the funds deposited, which can be withdrawn or left in the account to accumulate additional interest. The depositor also expects to be able to withdraw the principal, the original amount invested. These are the same types of considerations that guide investments in real estate.

The overall rate of return that the investor in real estate receives is called the **capitalization rate** or **overall capitalization rate.** In equation form, it can be expressed as:

$$\frac{\text{Net Operating Income}}{\text{Value}} = \text{Capitalization Rate}$$

or, $\dfrac{I}{V} = R$

The formula for the capitalization rate is particularly useful because of its two corollaries:

1. Capitalization Rate × Value = Net Operating Income

   or, $R \times V = I$

2. $\dfrac{\text{Net Operating Income}}{\text{Capitalization Rate}} = \text{Value}$

   or, $\dfrac{I}{R} = V$

Direct Capitalization

The capitalization rate can be developed by evaluating net income figures and sales prices of comparable properties. This process is called **direct capitalization.** For example, if a comparable property that sold recently for $250,000 produces an income of $25,000 per year, it has a capitalization rate of .10, or 10 percent, using the formula $\frac{I}{V} = R$, and dividing $25,000 by $250,000. To find the value of the subject property, the income that the appraiser estimates the subject property will produce is divided by the capitalization rate of ten percent. In this case, using the formula $\frac{I}{R} = V$, the subject property's income of $32,000 is divided by ten percent to derive a value estimate of $320,000.

Yield Capitalization

Yield capitalization is a way of analyzing both components of the capitalization rate (return *on* the investment and return *of* the investment) separately. It is too complex to discuss here, but is worth mentioning because it is likely to be the method of choice for analyzing a large-scale income-producing property.

Using yield capitalization, the appraiser selects a rate for the return on the investment, called the **discount rate** or **interest rate,** as well as a rate representing the return of the investment, called **capital recapture.** The discount rate will take into account the return required by the investor to produce a profit and can be found by using the **market extraction method** in which the discount rates of comparable properties are analyzed, or by the **band of investment method** in which the costs of carrying the financing necessary to make the investment are multiplied by the return required to make the carrying costs worthwhile.

SELECTING THE CAPITALIZATION TECHNIQUE

With the property's net operating income and the investor's desired capitalization rate determined, the appropriate capitalization technique must be selected and applied.

The appraiser first can determine the value of the underlying land by using the sales comparison approach, then apply the **building residual technique.** If the appraiser already has computed the building value, the calculations are reversed to find the total property value using the **land residual technique.** Using the **property residual technique,** the property is valued as a whole, including both land and buildings. A factor called an **annuity factor,** representing the present worth of an investment at the required yield, is multiplied by the net operating income to find the present worth of the income stream.

Figure 9.2 shows examples of how each of the capitalization techniques can be used. Note that each example makes use of a different property, with different income and other variables.

GROSS INCOME MULTIPLIER

Even though the income approach can be very detailed and can require a knowledge of sophisticated accounting techniques, a

FIGURE 9.2   Capitalization Techniques

Building Residual Technique

Estimated Land Value		$90,000
Net Operating Income	$40,000	
Discount on Land Value ($90,000 × .12)	−10,800	
Residual Income to Building	$29,200	
Capitalization Rate for Building		
Discount Rate 12%		
Recapture Rate + 5%		
17%		
Building Value ($29,200 ÷ .17)		171,800
Total Property Value		$261,800

Land Residual Technique

Assumed Building Value		$325,000
Net Operating Income	$65,000	
Capitalization Rate for Building		
Discount Rate 11.875%		
Recapture Rate + 4.000%		
15.875%		
Discount and Recapture on Building		
Value ($325,000 × .15875)	−51,600	
Residual Income to Land	$13,400	
Land Value ($13,400 ÷ .11875)		112,800
Total Property Value		$437,800

Property Residual Technique

Total Annual Net Operating Income	$40,000
Annuity Factor (23 years at 13%)	7.230
Present Worth of Net Operating Income	$289,200

much simpler form of income analysis can be used to make an estimate of the market value. As mentioned at the beginning of this chapter, the *gross income multiplier method* requires the appraiser to derive a factor based on the monthly rents and sales prices paid for properties comparable to the property being appraised. The factor, called the gross income multiplier (GIM), then can be multiplied by the income expected from the subject property to calculate the subject property's market value.

The formula to derive a gross income multiplier is:

$$\frac{\text{Sales Price}}{\text{Gross Income}} = \text{Gross Income Multiplier}$$

The formula to apply the gross income multiplier is:

Potential Gross Income × Gross Income Multiplier = Value

The gross income multiplier method often is used to appraise single-family residences. It serves as a check on the values reached by the sales comparison and cost approaches, however, rather than as the sole determinant of value.

For single-family residences, the gross income used will be the amount of the monthly rent, with no other source of income from the property. For this reason, this approach may be referred to as the **gross rent multiplier method.** When appraising commercial property, the amount of annual income from all sources is likely to include more than just rents, and the gross income multiplier is the more appropriate term.

The theory behind the use of the gross income multiplier is that rental prices and sales prices generally react to the same market influences, and so they tend to move in the same direction. Of course, not all factors will affect both rental prices and sales prices equally or at the same time. If property taxes go up, rents may rise well ahead of the time that the property taxed is sold. If a sudden drop in demand for rental units occurs because of overbuilding, rental prices and sales prices both will drop as new leases are begun and sales occur.

Some tenants are fortunate because they are paying rents based on the present owner's costs, which may be substantially less than those a new owner would incur to pay for the same property at today's prices. The appraiser should analyze the rental and sales prices of properties comparable to the property being appraised, keeping in mind the same economic factors that generally contribute to market value.

Figure 9.3 shows how a gross rent multiplier can be derived for a single-family residence and applied to the subject property to estimate market value. The appraiser's main concern will be to find comparable properties in the area that are being rented. Remember, too, that the appraiser must estimate a fair rental value for the subject property to apply the gross rent multiplier. This may be difficult if the property contains unique features that make it unlike others on the market.

FIGURE 9.3   Gross Rent Multiplier

Sale No.	Sales Price	Monthly Rental Income	Gross Rent Multiplier
1	$150,000	$ 975	154
2	145,000	975	149
3	152,000	1,000	152
4	140,000	875	160
5	160,000	1,100	145
Subject	?	1,000	?

In the example in Figure 9.3, the appraiser's gross rent multipliers range from 145 to 160. Discounting the high and low ends of the range, the remaining three figures are 149, 152 and 154. Based on the appraiser's knowledge of the properties involved and their similarities to the subject property, the multiplier of 152 is selected as being the most appropriate. The last step is to apply the gross rent multiplier to the estimated rental value of the subject:

$$\$1,000 \times 152 = \$152,000 \text{ Estimated Market Value}$$

APPRAISAL WORKSHEET

1. Is the subject property currently being rented and, if it is, what is the amount of the monthly rent? _____
2. Are comparable properties in the area currently being rented? _____
3. In the chart that follows, try to list at least five properties from the area that are comparable to the subject property, are used as rentals and have been sold recently.

Sale No.	Sales Price	Monthly Rental Income	Gross Rent Multiplier
1			
2			
3			
4			
5			

4. For each comparable property listed in the chart, divide the sales price by the amount of the monthly rent and enter the resulting gross rent multiplier in the chart.
5. Select the gross rent multiplier that is most appropriate for the subject property. _____
6. Based on the rents charged for properties comparable to the subject property, estimate the amount of rent that could be charged for the subject property. _____
7. Multiply the estimated rent for the property by the gross rent multiplier that you selected as most appropriate to find your estimate of market value. _____

10

Reconciliation and the Appraisal Report

The last step in the appraisal process, before the final report is prepared, is the reconciliation of the values indicated by each of the three appraisal approaches. Using the cost approach, the cost of reproducing or replacing the structure less depreciation plus site value has been calculated. With the income approach, value has been based on income the property should be capable of producing. With the sales comparison approach, the analysis of comparable sales produced adjusted sales prices that were used to derive an estimate of value for the subject property.

RECONCILIATION

The value estimates reached by using the different approaches rarely will be exactly the same. Even if the appraiser had all the relevant data and had carried out the steps in each approach without error, each value indication, in almost every case, would be different. In the **reconciliation** process, the validity of the methods and the result of each approach are weighed objectively to arrive at the single best and most supportable conclusion of value. This process also is called **correlation.**

In reconciling, or correlating, the appraiser reviews his or her work and considers at least four factors, including the:

1. Definition of value sought;
2. Amount and reliability of the data collected in each approach;
3. Inherent strengths and weaknesses of each approach; and
4. Relevance of each approach to the subject property and market behavior.

The process of reconciliation is not a simple averaging of the differing value estimates. After the factors listed previously are considered, the most relevant approach—cost, sales comparison or income—receives the greatest weight when determining the value estimate that most accurately reflects the value sought. In addition, each approach serves as a check against the others.

Review of the Three Approaches

To begin the reconciliation process, the appraiser reviews the steps followed in each approach to substantiate the accuracy and consistency of all data and the logic leading to the value estimate. The checklists in Figures 10.1 to 10.4 can be used to review each valuation approach.

Weighing the Choices

Once the appraiser is assured of the validity of the value estimates, he or she must decide which is the most reliable, in terms of the value sought, for the subject property. Inherent factors may make a particular method automatically more significant for certain kinds of property (such as the income approach for investment properties or the cost approach for special purpose properties). But other factors, of which the appraiser should be aware, may negate part of that significance. An unstable neighborhood, for instance, may make any structure virtually worthless. If the appraiser is trying to arrive at an estimate of the market value, and if the market for property in a certain neighborhood is likely to be extremely small, the appraiser should reflect this fact in his or her final value estimate.

FIGURE 10.1   Checklist for Sales Comparison Approach

Check:

_____ 1. That properties selected as comparables are sufficiently similar to the subject property;

_____ 2. Amount and reliability of sales data;

_____ 3. Factors used in comparison;

_____ 4. Logic of the adjustments made between comparable sales properties and the subject property;

_____ 5. Soundness of the value estimate drawn from the adjusted sales prices of comparable properties; and

_____ 6. Mathematical accuracy of the adjustment computations.

A check of all mathematical calculations is an important part of the review process because errors can lead to incorrect value indications and can destroy the credibility of the entire appraisal.

FIGURE 10.2 Checklist for Cost Approach

Check:

____ 1. That sites used as comparables are, in fact, similar to the subject site;
____ 2. Amount and reliability of the comparable sales data collected;
____ 3. Appropriateness of the factors used in comparison;
____ 4. Logic of the adjustments made between comparable sales sites and the subject site;
____ 5. Soundness of the value estimate drawn from the adjusted sales prices of comparable sites;
____ 6. Mathematical accuracy of the adjustment computations;
____ 7. Appropriateness of the method of estimating reproduction or replacement cost;
____ 8. Appropriateness of the unit cost factor;
____ 9. Accuracy of the reproduction or replacement cost computations;
____ 10. Market values assigned to accrued depreciation charges; and
____ 11. For double-counting and/or omissions in making accrued depreciation charges.

FIGURE 10.3 Checklist for Income Capitalization Approach

Check the logic and the mathematical accuracy of the:

____ 1. Market rents;
____ 2. Potential gross income estimate;
____ 3. Allowance for vacancy and collection losses;
____ 4. Operating expense estimate, including reserves for replacement;
____ 5. Net income estimate;
____ 6. Estimate of remaining economic life; and
____ 7. Capitalization rate and method of capitalizing.

FIGURE 10.4 Checklist for Gross Rent Multiplier Method

Check:

____ 1. That properties analyzed are comparable to the subject property and to one another in terms of locational, physical and investment characteristics;
____ 2. That adequate rental data is available;
____ 3. That comparable sales were drawn from properties that were rented at the time of sale;
____ 4. That the gross rent multiplier for the subject property was derived from current sales and current rental incomes; and
____ 5. Mathematical accuracy of all computations.

EXAMPLE:

An appraiser estimating the market value of a home in a neighborhood composed predominantly of owner-occupied single-family houses arrived at the following initial estimates:

Sales comparison approach	$165,750
Cost approach	169,500
Income approach	167,400

Based on these indications of value, the range is from $165,750 to $169,500, a difference of $3,750 between the lowest indication of value and the highest. This relatively narrow range suggests that the information gathered and analyzed is both a reasonable and reliable representation of the market.

When reviewing the data collected for the sales comparison approach and the results drawn, the appraiser realized that this value estimate should be very reliable. Other houses in the same general condition, and with the same types of improvements, were selling from $162,000 to $171,000. Because all comparable sales used in the analysis required few adjustments, considerable weight was given to the sales comparison approach as normally would be expected. After allowing for specific differences, an indicated value of $165,750 was determined for the subject property by applying the sales comparison approach.

Next, the appraiser analyzed the information collected and the result obtained using the cost approach. The cost approach tends to set an upper limit of value when the property is new, without functional or external obsolescence and at its highest and best use. The older a structure becomes, however, the more difficult it is to accurately estimate the proper amount of accrued depreciation. The fact that the house is relatively new, only a few years old, strengthens the $169,500 estimate of value by the cost approach.

Finally, the appraiser considered the market value derived from the income approach. This approach seemed to be the least valid for this particular property because few houses in the subject neighborhood are rentals and even fewer rental homes currently have been sold, making it difficult to establish a reasonably accurate gross rent multiplier.

As stated previously, the final value estimate is not an average but an opinion that the appraiser makes based on the type of property being appraised, the results of the research compiled and the valuation techniques used. In this case, the appraiser placed the most weight on the sales comparison approach.

The final value estimate should be rounded off to show that the number is, in fact, an estimate and not an exact or precise calculation. Thus, the appraiser's estimate of market value is $166,000—*not* $165,750.

Summary

The reconciliation process can be summarized best by a discussion of what it is *not*. Value reconciliation is *not* the correction of errors in thinking and technique. Any corrections to be made actually are part of the review process that preceded the final conclusion of value. The appraiser reconsiders the reasons for the various choices that were made throughout the appraisal framework as they affect the value estimates reached by the three approaches.

No formula exists for reconciling the various indicated values. Rather, reconciliation involves applying careful analysis and judgment for which no mathematical or mechanical formula can be substituted.

Reconciliation also is not merely a matter of averaging the three value estimates. Using a simple arithmetical average implies that the data and logic applied in each of the three approaches are equally reliable and therefore should be given equal weight. Certain approaches obviously are more valid and reliable with some kinds of properties than with others.

Finally, value reconciliation is not a narrowing of the range of value estimates. The value estimates developed from each approach never are changed—unless an error is found. Reconciliation is the final statement of reasoning and weighing of the relative importance of the facts, results and conclusions of each of the approaches that culminates in a fully justified final estimate of market value.

TYPES OF APPRAISAL REPORTS

The appraiser can report the final estimate of value to the client in several ways. The simplest is the **letter of opinion** that states only the appraiser's conclusion of value or often a range of value. The letter of opinion has limited use, however, because it provides neither supporting data nor the appraiser's analysis to the client.

A **form report** makes use of a standard form to provide, in a few pages, a synopsis of the data supporting the conclusion of value. The report form usually is accompanied by one or more exhibits depicting the subject property and its comparables. The type of property as well as the definition of the value sought will determine the exact form to be used.

In the secondary mortgage market created by government agencies and private organizations, form reports are required for

FIGURE 10.5   Uniform Residential Appraisal Report Form

UNIFORM RESIDENTIAL APPRAISAL REPORT File No.

Property Description

| Property Address | | City | | State | Zip Code |

Legal Description

County

Assessor's Parcel No. | Tax Year | R.E. Taxes $ | Special Assessments $

Borrower | Current Owner | Occupant: ☐ Owner ☐ Tenant ☐ Vacant

Property rights appraised ☐ Fee Simple ☐ Leasehold | Project Type ☐ PUD ☐ Condominium (HUD/VA only) | HOA$ /Mo.

Neighborhood or Project Name | Map Reference | Census Tract

Sale Price $ | Date of Sale | Description and $ amount of loan charges/concessions to be paid by seller

Lender/Client | Address

Appraiser | Address

Location	☐ Urban	☐ Suburban	☐ Rural	Predominant occupancy	Single family housing	Present land use %	Land use change
Built up	☐ Over 75%	☐ 25-75%	☐ Under 25%		PRICE $(000) AGE (yrs)	One family	☐ Not likely ☐ Likely
Growth rate	☐ Rapid	☐ Stable	☐ Slow	☐ Owner	Low	2-4 family	☐ In process
Property values	☐ Increasing	☐ Stable	☐ Declining	☐ Tenant	High	Multi-family	To:
Demand/supply	☐ Shortage	☐ In balance	☐ Over supply	☐ Vacant (0-5%)	Predominant	Commercial	
Marketing time	☐ Under 3 mos.	☐ 3-6 mos.	☐ Over 6 mos.	☐ Vacant (over 5%)			

Note: Race and the racial composition of the neighborhood are not appraisal factors.

Neighborhood boundaries and characteristics:

Factors that affect the marketability of the properties in the neighborhood (proximity to employment and amenities, employment stability, appeal to market, etc.):

Market conditions in the subject neighborhood (including support for the above conclusions related to the trend of property values, demand/supply, and marketing time - - such as data on competitive properties for sale in the neighborhood, description of the prevalence of sales and financing concessions, etc.):

Project Information for PUDs (If applicable) - - Is the developer/builder in control of the Home Owners' Association (HOA)? ☐ Yes ☐ No

Approximate total number of units in the subject project_____ Approximate total number of units for sale in the subject project_____

Describe common elements and recreational facilities:

Dimensions _____ | Topography _____

Site area _____ Corner Lot ☐ Yes ☐ No | Size _____

Specific zoning classification and description _____ | Shape _____

Zoning compliance ☐ Legal ☐ Legal nonconforming (Grandfathered use) ☐ Illegal ☐ No zoning | Drainage _____

Highest & best use as improved: ☐ Present use ☐ Other use (explain) | View _____

Utilities	Public	Other	Off-site Improvements	Type	Public	Private	Landscaping _____
Electricity			Street				Driveway Surface _____
Gas			Curb/gutter				Apparent easements _____
Water			Sidewalk				FEMA Special Flood Hazard Area ☐ Yes ☐ No
Sanitary sewer			Street lights				FEMA Zone _____ Map Date _____
Storm sewer			Alley				FEMA Map No.

Comments (apparent adverse easements, encroachments, special assessments, slide areas, illegal or legal nonconforming zoning use, etc.):

GENERAL DESCRIPTION	EXTERIOR DESCRIPTION	FOUNDATION	BASEMENT	INSULATION
No. of Units	Foundation	Slab	Area Sq. Ft.	Roof ☐
No. of Stories	Exterior Walls	Crawl Space	% Finished	Ceiling ☐
Type (Det./Att.)	Roof Surface	Basement	Ceiling	Walls ☐
Design (Style)	Gutters & Dwnspts.	Sump Pump	Walls	Floor ☐
Existing/Proposed	Window Type	Dampness	Floor	None ☐
Age (Yrs.)	Storm/Screens	Settlement	Outside Entry	Unknown ☐
Effective Age (Yrs.)	Manufactured House	Infestation		

ROOMS	Foyer	Living	Dining	Kitchen	Den	Family Rm.	Rec. Rm.	Bedrooms	# Baths	Laundry	Other	Area Sq. Ft.
Basement												
Level 1												
Level 2												

Finished area **above** grade contains: _____ Rooms; _____ Bedroom(s); _____ Bath(s); _____ Square Feet of Gross Living Area

INTERIOR	Materials/Condition	HEATING		KITCHEN EQUIP.		ATTIC		AMENITIES		CAR STORAGE:	
Floors		Type		Refrigerator		None		Fireplace(s) #		None ☐	
Walls		Fuel		Range/Oven		Stairs		Patio		Garage	# of cars
Trim/Finish		Condition		Disposal		Drop Stair		Deck		Attached	
Bath Floor		COOLING		Dishwasher		Scuttle		Porch		Detached	
Bath Wainscot		Central		Fan/Hood		Floor		Fence		Built-In	
Doors		Other		Microwave		Heated		Pool		Carport	
		Condition		Washer/Dryer		Finished				Driveway	

Additional features (special energy efficient items, etc.):

Condition of the improvements, depreciation (physical, functional, and external), repairs needed, quality of construction, remodeling/additions, etc.:

Adverse environmental conditions (such as, but not limited to, hazardous wastes, toxic substances, etc.) present in the improvements, on the site, or in the immediate vicinity of the subject property.:

Freddie Mac Form 70   6-93   10 CH.   PAGE 1 OF 2   U.S. Forms, Inc. 1-800-225-9583   Fannie Mae Form 1004 6-93

USF# 00110

FIGURE 10.5 Uniform Residential Appraisal Report Form (Continued)

UNIFORM RESIDENTIAL APPRAISAL REPORT   File No. _____

Valuation Section

COST APPROACH

ESTIMATED SITE VALUE . . . . = $ _____
ESTIMATED REPRODUCTION COST-NEW-OF IMPROVEMENTS:
Dwelling _____ Sq. Ft @ $ _____ = $ _____
_____ Sq. Ft @ $ _____ = _____
= _____
Garage/Carport_____ Sq. Ft @ $ _____ = _____
Total Estimated Cost New . . . . = $ _____
Less   Physical   Functional   External
Depreciation _____ = $ _____
Depreciated Value of Improvements . . . . = $ _____
"As-is" Value of Site Improvements . . . . = $ _____
INDICATED VALUE BY COST APPROACH . . . . = $ _____

Comments on Cost Approach (such as, source of cost estimate, site value, square foot calculation and for HUD, VA and FmHA, the estimated remaining economic life of the property): _____
_____
_____
_____
_____
_____
_____
_____

SALES COMPARISON ANALYSIS

ITEM	SUBJECT	COMPARABLE NO. 1		COMPARABLE NO. 2		COMPARABLE NO. 3	
Address							
Proximity to Subject							
Sales Price	$		$		$		$
Price/Gross Liv. Area	$ ⊘	$ ⊘		$ ⊘		$ ⊘	
Data and/or Verification Source							
VALUE ADJUSTMENTS	DESCRIPTION	DESCRIPTION	+ (-) $ Adjustment	DESCRIPTION	+ (-) $ Adjustment	DESCRIPTION	+ (-) $ Adjustment
Sales or Financing Concessions							
Date of Sale/Time							
Location							
Leasehold/Fee Simple							
Site							
View							
Design and Appeal							
Quality of Construction							
Age							
Condition							
Above Grade	Total ¦ Bdrms ¦ Baths	Total ¦ Bdrms ¦ Baths		Total ¦ Bdrms ¦ Baths		Total ¦ Bdrms ¦ Baths	
Room Count	¦ ¦	¦ ¦		¦ ¦		¦ ¦	
Gross Living Area	Sq. Ft.	Sq. Ft.		Sq. Ft.		Sq. Ft.	
Basement & Finished Rooms Below Grade							
Functional Utility							
Heating/Cooling							
Energy Efficient Items							
Garage/Carport							
Porch, Patio, Deck, Fireplace(s), etc.							
Fence, Pool, etc.							
Net Adj. (total)		☐ + ☐ - $		☐ + ☐ - $		☐ + ☐ - $	
Adjusted Sales Price of Comparable			$		$		$

Comments on Sales Comparison (including the subject property's compatibility to the neighborhood, etc.): _____
_____
_____
_____
_____

ITEM	SUBJECT	COMPARABLE NO. 1	COMPARABLE NO. 2	COMPARABLE NO. 3
Date, Price and Data Source, for prior sales within year of appraisal				

Analysis of any current agreement of sale, option, or listing of the subject property and analysis of any prior sales of subject and comparables within one year of the date of appraisal:
_____
_____

INDICATED VALUE BY SALES COMPARISON APPROACH . . . . $ _____
INDICATED VALUE BY INCOME APPROACH (If Applicable) Estimated Market Rent $ _____ /Mo. x Gross Rent Multiplier _____ = $ _____

RECONCILIATION

This appraisal is made ☐ "as is" ☐ subject to the repairs, alterations, inspections or conditions listed below ☐ subject to completion per plans and specifications.
Conditions of Appraisal:_____
_____
Final Reconciliation: _____
_____
_____

The purpose of this appraisal is to estimate the market value of the real property that is the subject of this report, based on the above conditions and the certification, contingent and limiting conditions, and market value definition that are stated in the attached Freddie Mac Form 439/Fannie Mae Form 1004B (Revised _____).
I (WE) ESTIMATE THE MARKET VALUE, AS DEFINED, OF THE REAL PROPERTY THAT IS THE SUBJECT OF THIS REPORT, AS OF _____
(WHICH IS THE DATE OF INSPECTION AND THE EFFECTIVE DATE OF THIS REPORT) TO BE $ _____

APPRAISER:	SUPERVISORY APPRAISER (ONLY IF REQUIRED):.	
Signature _____	Signature _____	☐ Did ☐ Did Not
Name _____	Name _____	Inspect Property
Date Report Signed _____	Date Report Signed _____	
State Certification # _____ State	State Certification # _____ State	
Or State License # _____ State	Or State License # _____ State	

Freddie Mac Form 70   6-93   10 CH.   PAGE 2 OF 2   Fannie Mae Form 1004 6-93 the purchase and sale of most existing mortgages on residential properties. Figure 10.5 shows the two-page Uniform Residential Appraisal Report (URAR) form commonly used by appraisers when valuing homes.

The most thorough presentation of the appraiser's assumptions, data, analyses, findings and conclusions is provided in a **narrative appraisal report.** In a narrative appraisal report, the appraiser summarizes the important background research and presents all the relevant data for each appraisal method that contributed to the final estimate of value. A number of exhibits may be included, such as photographs of the subject property and its comparables and maps showing demographic, topographical, soil and other analyses of the subject and its comparables. Narrative reports can contain just a few pages to several hundred pages.

Every appraisal report, regardless of its length, should contain the following:

1. Name of person for whom the report is made;
2. Date of appraisal;
3. Identification and description of the property;
4. Purpose of the appraisal;
5. Value conclusion; and
6. Appraiser's certification and signature.

FINAL COMMENT

It should be obvious to the reader that an appraiser is not a magician and does not consult a crystal ball to forecast property value. Figure 10.6 shows a one-page addendum that was drafted to accompany the Uniform Residential Appraisal Report form. It is used to define the appraiser's task and temper the client's expectations. Similar wording typically appears on other types of appraisal reports as well.

Remember that an appraisal is not an exercise in stargazing or fortune-telling, but a process that should lead to a well-reasoned judgment based on available facts.

FIGURE 10.6   Addendum to the Uniform Residential Appraisal Report Form

DEFINITION OF MARKET VALUE: The most probable price which a property should bring in a competitive and open market under all conditions requisite to a fair sale, the buyer and seller, each acting prudently, knowledgeably and assuming the price is not affected by undue stimulus. Implicit in this definition is the consummation of a sale as of a specified date and the passing of title from seller to buyer under conditions whereby: (1) buyer and seller are typically motivated; (2) both parties are well informed or well advised, and each acting in what he considers his own best interest; (3) a reasonable time is allowed for exposure in the open market; (4) payment is made in terms of cash in U.S. dollars or in terms of financial arrangements comparable thereto; and (5) the price represents the normal consideration for the property sold unaffected by special or creative financing or sales concessions* granted by anyone associated with the sale.

*Adjustments to the comparables must be made for special or creative financing or sales concessions. No adjustments are necessary for those costs which are normally paid by sellers as a result of tradition or law in a market area; these costs are readily identifiable since the seller pays these costs in virtually all sales transactions. Special or creative financing adjustments can be made to the comparable property by comparisons to financing terms offered by a third party institutional lender that is not already involved in the property or transaction. Any adjustment should not be calculated on a mechanical dollar for dollar cost of the financing or concession but the dollar amount of any adjustment should approximate the market's reaction to the financing or concessions based on the appraiser's judgment.

CERTIFICATION AND STATEMENT OF LIMITING CONDITIONS

CERTIFICATION: The Appraiser certifies and agrees that:

1. The Appraiser has no present or contemplated future interest in the property appraised; and neither the employment to make the appraisal, nor the compensation for it, is contingent upon the appraised value of the property.

2. The Appraiser has no personal interest in or bias with respect to the subject matter of the appraisal report or the participants to the sale. The "Estimate of Market Value" in the appraisal report is not based in whole or in part upon the race, color, or national origin of the prospective owners or occupants of the property appraised, or upon the race, color or national origin of the present owners or occupants of the properties in the vicinity of the property appraised.

3. The Appraiser has personally inspected the property, both inside and out, and has made an exterior inspection of all comparable sales listed in the report. To the best of the Appraiser's knowledge and belief, all statements and information in this report are true and correct, and the Appraiser has not knowingly withheld any significant information.

4. All contingent and limiting conditions are contained herein (imposed by the terms of the assignment or by the undersigned affecting the analyses, opinions, and conclusions contained in the report).

5. This appraisal report has been made in conformity with and is subject to the requirements of the Code of Professional Ethics and Standards of Professional Conduct of the appraisal organizations with which the Appraiser is affiliated.

6. All conclusions and opinions concerning the real estate that are set forth in the appraisal report were prepared by the Appraiser whose signature appears on the appraisal report, unless indicated as "Review Appraiser." No change of any item in the appraisal report shall be made by anyone other than the Appraiser, and the Appraiser shall have no responsibility for any such unauthorized change.

CONTINGENT AND LIMITING CONDITIONS: The certification of the Appraiser appearing in the appraisal report is subject to the following conditions and to such other specific and limiting conditions as are set forth by the Appraiser in the report.

1. The Appraiser assumes no responsibility for matters of a legal nature affecting the property appraised or the title thereto, nor does the Appraiser render any opinion as to the title, which is assumed to be good and marketable. The property is appraised as though under responsible ownership.

2. Any sketch in the report may show approximate dimensions and is included to assist the reader in visualizing the property. The Appraiser has made no survey of the property.

3. The Appraiser is not required to give testimony or appear in court because of having made the appraisal with reference to the property in question, unless arrangements have been previously made therefor.

4. Any distribution of the valuation in the report between land and improvements applies only under the existing program of utilization. The separate valuations for land and building must not be used in conjunction with any other appraisal and are invalid if so used.

5. The Appraiser assumes that there are no hidden or unapparent conditions of the property, subsoil, or structures, which would render it more or less valuable. The Appraiser assumes no responsibility for such conditions, or for engineering which might be required to discover such factors.

6. Information, estimates, and opinions furnished to the Appraiser, and contained in the report, were obtained from sources considered reliable and believed to be true and correct. However, no responsibility for accuracy of such items furnished the Appraiser can be assumed by the Appraiser.

7. Disclosure of the contents of the appraisal report is governed by the Bylaws and Regulations of the professional appraisal organizations with which the Appraiser is affiliated.

8. Neither all, nor any part of the content of the report, or copy thereof (including conclusions as to the property value, the identity of the Appraiser, professional designations, reference to any professional appraisal organizations, or the firm with which the Appraiser is connected), shall be used for any purposes by anyone but the client specified in the report, the borrower if appraisal fee paid by same, the mortgagee or its successors and assigns, mortgage insurers, consultants, professional appraisal organizations, any state or federally approved financial institution, any department, agency, or instrumentality of the United States or any state or the District of Columbia, without the previous written consent of the Appraiser; nor shall it be conveyed by anyone to the public through advertising, public relations, news, sales, or other media, without the written consent and approval of the Appraiser.

9. On all appraisals, subject to satisfactory completion, repairs, or alterations, the appraisal report and value conclusion are contingent upon completion of the improvements in a workmanlike manner.

Date: _____   Appraiser(s) _____

FREDDIE MAC
FORM 439 JUL 86   U.S. Forms Inc., 2 Central Sq., Grafton, MA 01519-0446   1-800-225-9583   1-839-4417   FANNIE MAE
USF 00600   FORM 1004B JUL 86

Appendix A: Calculating Area

A home appraisal generally requires the use of area in some way. Area is given in square units. When comparing properties, for example, you must be able to determine the size of a lot in square feet, the amount of floor space in a room or house and the construction cost per square foot of various components of the house.

Many property boundaries and houses are irregularly shaped; that is, they are not rectangular. This appendix will show you how to compute the area of just about any shape that you might encounter.

AREA OF SQUARES AND RECTANGLES

The space inside a two-dimensional shape is its *area*. A *right angle* is the angle formed by one-fourth of a circle. Because a full circle is 360°, and one-fourth of 360° is 90°, a right angle is a 90° angle.

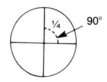

Squares and Rectangles

A *rectangle* is a closed figure with four sides that are at right angles to each other.

A *square* is a rectangle with four sides of equal length. A square with four sides, each one inch long, is a *square inch*. A square with four sides, each one foot long, is a *square foot*.

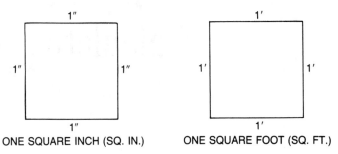

ONE SQUARE INCH (SQ. IN.)   ONE SQUARE FOOT (SQ. FT.)

Note: The symbol for *inch* is ". The symbol for *foot* is '. The abbreviations are *in.* and *ft.*

The area of a shape is the number of *square units* inside the shape. One way to find the number of square units in a shape is to place the shape on a larger number of square units and count the number of square units inside the shape.

The area of the square at the left, below, is four square inches.

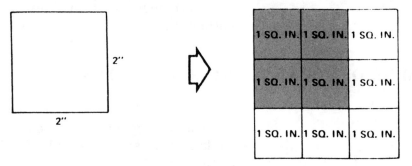

Counting squares is too cumbersome a method to use when dealing with large areas. The following formula may be used to compute the area of any rectangle:

$$area = length \times width, \text{ or}$$
$$A = L \times W$$

The area of the following rectangle, using the formula, is $5'' \times 6''$, or 30 square inches.

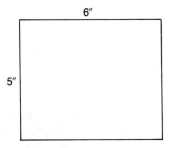

The term *30 inches* refers to a straight line 30 inches long. The term *30 square inches* refers to the area of a specific figure. When inches are multiplied by inches, the answer will be in square inches. Likewise, when feet are multiplied by feet, the answer will be in square feet.

Square feet are sometimes expressed by using the exponent, two; for example, 10^2 is read 10 feet squared and means 10×10, or 100 square feet.

The exponent ^{2} indicates how many times the number, or unit of measurement, is multiplied by itself. This is called the *power* of the number or unit of measurement. The exponent is indicated at the upper right of the original number or unit of measurement.

The area of the rectangle at the left, below, is $4' \times 6'$, or 24 square feet. The area of the square at the right, below, is 5 yards $\times$ 5 yards, or 25 square yards.

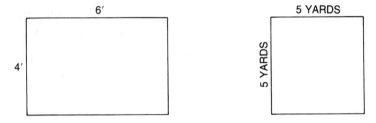

EXAMPLE:

Mr. Blair has leased a vacant lot that measures 60 by 160 feet. How much rent will he pay per year if the lot rents for $.35 per square foot per year?

Solution: To solve this problem, first compute the area of the lot:

$$A = L \times W = 160' \times 60' = 9,600 \text{ sq. ft.}$$

Then multiply the number of square feet by the price per square foot to calculate the total rent:

$$9,600 \times \$.35 = \$3,360$$

CONVERSIONS—USING LIKE MEASURES FOR AREA

When area is computed, all the dimensions used must be given in the *same kind of units*. When a formula is used to find area, units of the same kind must be used for each element of the formula, with the answer as square units of that kind. So inches must be multiplied by inches to arrive at square inches; feet must be multiplied by feet to arrive at square feet; and yards must be multiplied by yards to arrive at square yards.

If the two dimensions to be multiplied are in different units of measure, one of the units of measure must be converted to the other. The following chart shows how to make these conversions:

$$12 \text{ inches } = 1 \text{ foot}$$
$$36 \text{ inches } = 1 \text{ yard}$$
$$3 \text{ feet } = 1 \text{ yard}$$

To convert *feet* to *inches*,
multiply the number of feet by 12.   (*ft.* × 12 = in.)

To convert *inches* to *feet*,
divide the number of inches by 12.   (*in.* ÷ 12 = ft.)

To convert *yards* to *feet*,
multiply the number of yards by 3.   (*yd.* × 3 = ft.)

To convert *feet* to *yards*,
divide the number of feet by 3.   (*ft.* ÷ 3 = yd.)

To convert *yards* to *inches*,
multiply the number of yards by 36.   (*yd.* × 36 = in.)

To convert *inches* to *yards*,
divide the number of inches by 36.   (*in.* ÷ 36 = yd.)

EXAMPLE:

Ms. Johnson's house is on a lot that is 75 feet by 1,500 inches. What is the area of the lot?

Solution: To solve this problem, first convert inches to feet:

$$1,500 \text{ inches } \div 12 = 125 \text{ feet}$$

Then compute the area of the lot:

$$A = L \times W = 75' \times 125' = 9,375 \text{ square feet}$$

To convert square inches, square feet and square yards, use the following chart:

To convert *square feet* to *square inches*,
multiply the number of square feet by 144.   (*sq. ft.* × 144 = sq. in.)

To convert *square inches* to *square feet*,
divide the number of square inches by 144.   (*sq. in.* ÷ 144 = sq. ft.)

To convert *square yards* to *square feet*,
multiply the number of square yards by 9.   (*sq. yd.* × 9 = sq. ft.)

To convert *square feet* to *square yards*,
divide the number of square feet by 9.   (*sq. ft.* ÷ 9 = sq. yd.)

To convert *square yards* to *square inches*,
multiply the number of square yards by   (*sq. yd.* × 1,296
1,296.   = sq. in.)

To convert *square inches* to *square yards*,
divide the number of square inches by   (*sq. in.* ÷ 1,296
1,296.   = sq. yd.)

AREA OF TRIANGLES

A *triangle* is a closed figure with three straight sides and three angles. *Tri* means three.

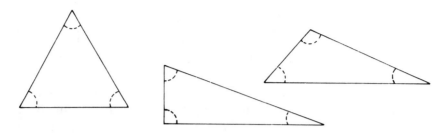

The square-inch figure at the left, below, has been cut in half by a straight line drawn through its opposite corners to make two equal triangles. When one of the triangles is placed on a square-inch grid, it is seen to contain ½ sq. in. + ½ sq. in. + 1 sq. in., or 2 sq. in.

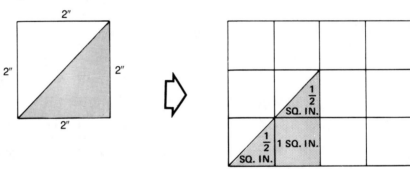

The area of the triangle below is 4.5 sq. ft.

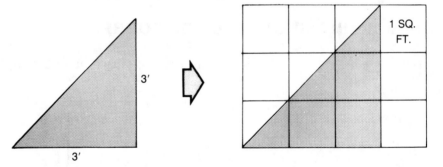

Again, the square-unit grid is too cumbersome for computing large areas. It is more convenient to use a formula for finding the area of a triangle:

$$\text{area of a triangle} = \tfrac{1}{2}\,(\text{base} \times \text{height}), \text{ or}$$
$$A = \tfrac{1}{2}\,(BH)$$

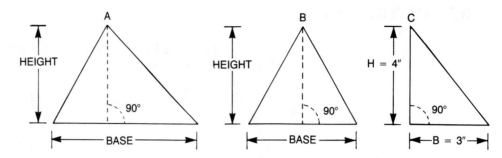

The *base* is the side on which the triangle sits. The *height* is the straight-line distance from the tip of the uppermost angle to the base. The height must form a 90° angle to the base. The area of triangle *C* above is:

$$A = \tfrac{1}{2}(BH) = \tfrac{1}{2}(3'' \times 4'') = \tfrac{1}{2}(12 \text{ sq. in.}) = 6 \text{ sq. in.}$$

EXAMPLE:

The diagram below shows a lakefront lot. Compute its area.

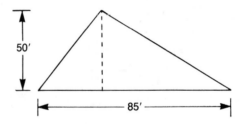

Solution: $A = \tfrac{1}{2}(BH) = \tfrac{1}{2}(50' \times 85') = \tfrac{1}{2}(4{,}250$ sq. ft.$) = 2{,}125$ sq. ft.

AREA OF IRREGULAR CLOSED FIGURES

Here is a drawing of two neighboring lots:

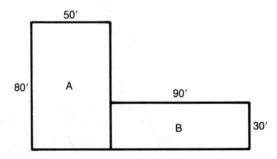

To find the total area of both lots:

lot $A = 50' \times 80' = 4{,}000$ sq. ft.
lot $B = 90' \times 30' = 2{,}700$ sq. ft.
both lots $= 4{,}000$ sq. ft. $+ 2{,}700$ sq. ft. $= 6{,}700$ sq. ft.

Two rectangles can be made by drawing one straight line inside figure *1*, below. There are two possible positions for the added line, as shown in figures *2* and *3*.

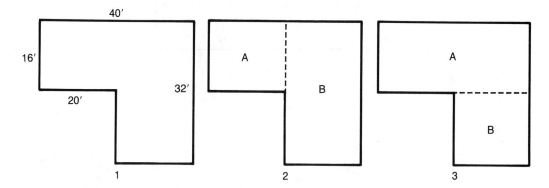

Using the measurements given in figure *1*, the total area of the figure may be computed in one of two ways:

Area of $A = 20' \times 16' = 320$ sq. ft.
Area of $B = 32' \times (40' - 20') = 32' \times 20' = 640$ sq. ft.
Total Area $= 320$ sq. ft. $+ 640$ sq. ft. $= 960$ sq. ft.

Or:

Area of $A = 40' \times 16' = 640$ sq. ft.
Area of $B = (40' - 20') \times (32' - 16') = 20' \times 16' = 320$ sq. ft.
Total Area $= 640$ sq. ft. $+ 320$ sq. ft. $= 960$ sq. ft.

The area of an irregular figure can be found by dividing it into regular figures, computing the area of each regular figure and adding all the areas together to obtain the total area.

EXAMPLE:

Compute the area of each section of the following figure. Then compute the total area.

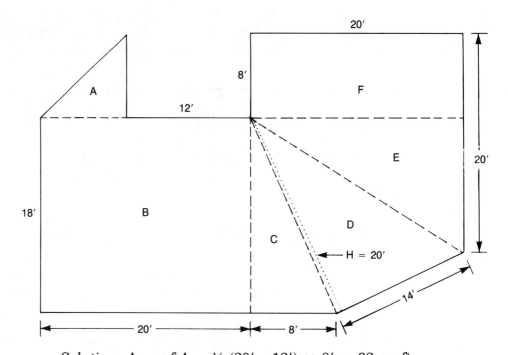

Solution: Area of $A = \frac{1}{2}(20' - 12') \times 8' = 32$ sq. ft.
Area of $B = 18' \times 20' = 360$ sq. ft.
Area of $C = \frac{1}{2}(8' \times 18') = 72$ sq. ft.
Area of $D = \frac{1}{2}(14' \times 20') = 140$ sq. ft.
Area of $E = \frac{1}{2}(20' - 8') \times 20' = 120$ sq. ft.
Area of $F = 8' \times 20' = 160$ sq. ft.

Total Area = 32 + 360 + 72 + 140 + 120 + 160 sq. ft. = 884 sq. ft.

LIVING-AREA CALCULATIONS

Real estate appraisers frequently must compute the amount of living area in a house. The living area of a house is the area enclosed by the outside dimensions of the heated and air-conditioned portions of the house that are entirely above grade. This *excludes* open porches, garages, basements (even when finished and heated), unfinished attics, etc.

When measuring a house to prepare for calculating the living area, these steps should be followed:

1. Draw a sketch of the foundation.
2. Measure *all* outside walls.
3. If the house has an attached garage, treat the inside garage walls that are common to the house as outside walls of the house.
4. Measure the garage.
5. Convert inches to tenths of a foot (so that the same units of measurement are used in the calculations).
6. Before leaving the house, check to see that net dimensions of opposite sides are equal. If not, remeasure.

7. Section off your sketch into rectangles.
8. Calculate the area of each rectangle.
9. Add up the areas, being careful to *subtract* the area of the garage, *if necessary*.
10. Before leaving the house, *always* recheck the dimensions.

EXAMPLE:

What is the living area of the house shown in the sketch below? Follow the steps listed as you read.

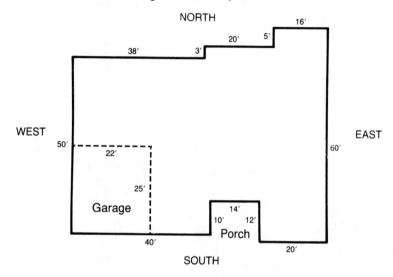

Area

Solution:
$$A = 5' \times 16' \qquad\qquad\qquad\quad = \quad 80 \text{ sq. ft.}$$
$$B = 3' \times (20' + 16') = 3' \times 36' \quad = \quad 108$$
$$C = 12' \times 20' \qquad\qquad\qquad\quad = \quad 240$$
$$D = 10' \times (40' - 22') = 10' \times 18' \quad = \quad 180$$
$$E = (50' - 25') \times 22' = 25' \times 22' \quad = \quad 550$$
$$F = (50' - 10') \times (74' - 22') = 40' \times 52' = \underline{2080}$$
$$\text{TOTAL} = 3238 \text{ sq. ft.}$$

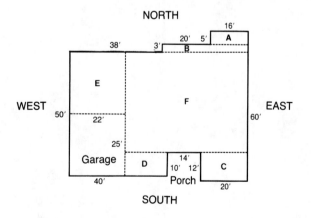

Appendix B:
The Value of Home Improvements

Remodeling can make a house more valuable as well as more livable. Although the cash invested in improvements seldom yields a dollar-for-dollar return when the house is sold, some remodelings do promise to return more of the investment than others. Keep in mind, however, that no matter how much is invested in improvements, ultimately it's the marketplace that determines what the home is worth.

Figure B.1 shows the payback potential of 20 popular remodelings.

FIGURE B.1   Remodeling Projects and How They Pay Off

	Type of Improvement	*Recovery Cost %*
1.	Room addition	70–90
2.	Major kitchen remodeling	45–70
3.	Minor kitchen remodeling	60–80
4.	New bath	75–100
5.	Bathroom remodeling	60–80
6.	Master suite	60–80
7.	Reroofing	10–30
8.	Finished basement	30–45
9.	Garage	30–50
10.	Windows and doors	25–45
11.	Insulation	0–25
12.	New heating system	30–45
13.	Deck	65–75
14.	Sunspace	5–20
15.	Swimming pool	varies by market
16.	Skylight	0–30
17.	Exterior painting	40–50
18.	Siding	15–35
19.	Landscaping	45–65
20.	Energy-efficient fireplace	75–100

Appendix C:
Anatomy of a House

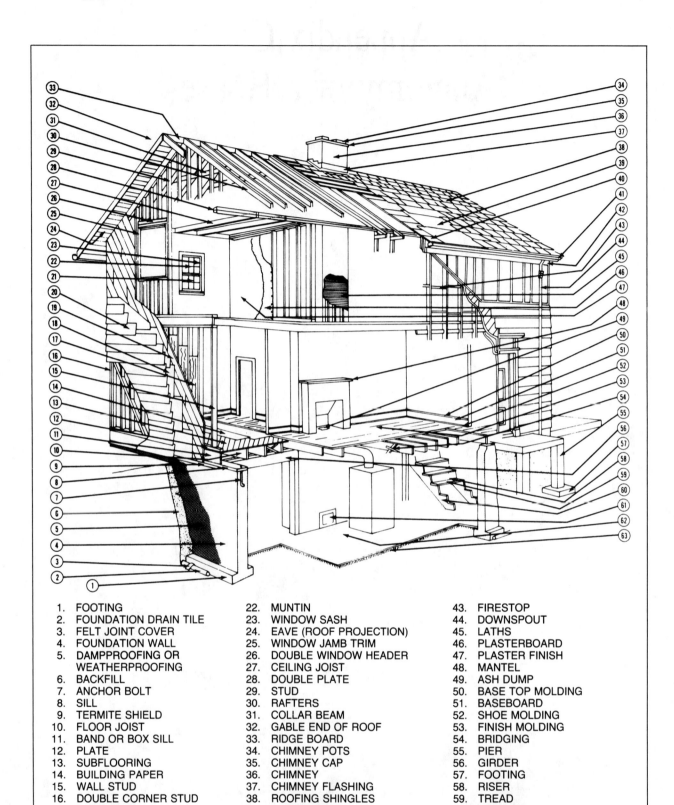

1. FOOTING	22. MUNTIN	43. FIRESTOP
2. FOUNDATION DRAIN TILE	23. WINDOW SASH	44. DOWNSPOUT
3. FELT JOINT COVER	24. EAVE (ROOF PROJECTION)	45. LATHS
4. FOUNDATION WALL	25. WINDOW JAMB TRIM	46. PLASTERBOARD
5. DAMPPROOFING OR WEATHERPROOFING	26. DOUBLE WINDOW HEADER	47. PLASTER FINISH
6. BACKFILL	27. CEILING JOIST	48. MANTEL
7. ANCHOR BOLT	28. DOUBLE PLATE	49. ASH DUMP
8. SILL	29. STUD	50. BASE TOP MOLDING
9. TERMITE SHIELD	30. RAFTERS	51. BASEBOARD
10. FLOOR JOIST	31. COLLAR BEAM	52. SHOE MOLDING
11. BAND OR BOX SILL	32. GABLE END OF ROOF	53. FINISH MOLDING
12. PLATE	33. RIDGE BOARD	54. BRIDGING
13. SUBFLOORING	34. CHIMNEY POTS	55. PIER
14. BUILDING PAPER	35. CHIMNEY CAP	56. GIRDER
15. WALL STUD	36. CHIMNEY	57. FOOTING
16. DOUBLE CORNER STUD	37. CHIMNEY FLASHING	58. RISER
17. INSULATION	38. ROOFING SHINGLES	59. TREAD
18. BUILDING PAPER	39. ROOFING FELTS	60. STRINGER
19. WALL SHEATHING	40. ROOF SHEATHING	61. CLEANOUT DOOR
20. SIDING	41. EAVE TROUGH OR GUTTER	62. CONCRETE BASEMENT FLOOR
21. MULLION	42. FRIEZE BOARD	63. CINDER FILL

Glossary

AACI Accredited Appraiser Canadian Institute.

AAE Accredited Assessment Evaluator, International Association of Assessing Officers.

Abatement The process by which an *ad valorem* real property tax assessment is stopped or reduced.

absolute fee simple title An unqualified right of ownership in real estate. Fee simple is the best title that can be possessed. Note that, even with fee simple title, there still may be some limitation on the use of the property. The limitation may be one that is publicly imposed, such as a zoning classification that allows only a stated property use, or the limitation may be privately imposed, such as a deed restriction that specifies architectural standards.

access The right to enter or leave a tract of land from a public way, which may be by an easement over land owned by someone else. Other terms that are used to refer to the right of access are *ingress* (right to enter) and *egress* (right to leave).

accessory buildings Structures that are secondary to the main building. On a residential lot, these might include a garage or storage shed.

accrued depreciation Total depreciation from the time of construction up to the time of appraisal.

accrued expenses Expenses incurred that are not yet payable.

acquisition appraisal An appraisal to determine the fair market value of property condemned for public use to establish the compensation to be paid to the property owner.

acre A measure of land with a perimeter of approximately 209 feet by 209 feet; in area, 43,560 square feet or 160 square rods or 4,840 square yards.

actual age The total number of years elapsed since a structure was built; also referred to as *historical* or *chronological age.*

adjustment Change to the sales price of a comparable property to account for a difference between the comparable and the property that is the subject of an appraisal. The sales price is increased by the value of any feature that is present in the subject but not in the comparable, but decreased by the value of any feature that is present in the comparable but not in the subject.

ad valorem Latin phrase meaning *according to value;* generally used to refer to any form of taxation based on the relative value of the things being taxed. Most real estate taxes are *ad valorem* taxes.

adverse land use A land use that has a detrimental effect on the market value of nearby properties.

aesthetic Relating to beauty, rather than to functional considerations.

AFA Association of Federal Appraisers.

age-life method   Another name for the straight-line method of computing accrued depreciation.

AI   Appraisal Institute.

AIC   Appraisal Institute of Canada.

air rights   The right to use the space above the physical surface of the land, generally allowing the surface to be used for some other purpose. Some air rights are transferable, allowing builders to combine air rights of several different properties to build a single high-rise structure.

allocation method   Separation of the appraised total value of real estate between land and building. Allocation may be made by using a ratio or by subtracting a figure representing building value from the total appraised value of the property.

allowance for vacancy and collection losses   The percentage of potential gross income that will be lost because of vacant units, collection losses or both.

amenities   In appraising, those property features that contribute to the owner's satisfaction and enjoyment of the property, particularly those benefits other than monetary, such as architectural excellence or scenic beauty.

anticipation, principle of   The principle that the selling price of real estate is affected by the expectation of its future appeal and value.

appraisal   An estimate of quantity, quality or value, and the process by which conclusions of property value are obtained. Also refers to the report setting forth the estimate of value and the process by which the estimate was reached.

appraisal methods   The approaches used in the appraisal of real estate, including the cost approach, income capitalization approach and sales comparison approach.

appraisal report   An appraiser's written opinion to a client of the value of the subject property sought as of the date of the appraisal. A *form report* gives the most important details of the appraisal process in only a few pages, while a *narrative report* provides a comprehensive analysis of the data used to reach the estimate of value.

appraiser   One who estimates value.

appreciation   Increase in monetary value over time.

arm's-length transaction   A transaction in which both the buyer and the seller act willingly and under no pressure, with knowledge of the present conditions and future potential of the property, and in which the property has been offered on the open market for a reasonable length of time and no unusual financing or other circumstances exist.

ASA   American Society of Appraisers.

assessed value   The value placed on land and buildings by a government entity (usually, the assessor) for use in levying real estate taxes.

assessment   The imposition of a tax, charge or levy, usually according to established rates.

assessor   The governmental official who determines property values for the purpose of *ad valorem* taxation, that is, taxation based on the relative value of property.

balance, principle of   As applied to property uses, the principle that properties can reach their highest value when there are a sufficient number of complementary property types in the area; for instance, when the number of residential properties is adequate for the available retail facilities. A market is said to be in balance when there are somewhat more properties available for sale than there are buyers.

base rent　The minimum rent payable under a percentage lease.

book value　The value of a property as capital on the books of account; usually reproduction or replacement cost, plus additions to capital and less reserves for depreciation.

building capitalization rate　The sum of the discount and capital recovery rates for a building.

building codes　State laws or local ordinances specifying minimum building construction standards for the protection of public health and safety.

building residual technique　A method of income capitalization using the net income remaining to the building after interest on land value has been deducted.

bundle of rights　A term often applied to the rights of ownership of real estate, including the rights of using, renting, selling or giving away the real estate or not taking any of these actions.

CAE　Certified Assessment Evaluator, International Association of Assessing Officers.

capital　Money or goods used to acquire other money or goods.

capitalization　Estimating the value of real estate by applying a desired rate of return to the property's expected annual net operating income, expressed as a formula:

$$\frac{\text{Income}}{\text{Rate}} = \text{Value}$$

capitalization rate　The rate that includes both a return on an investment as well as the return of the amount invested.

capitalized value method of depreciation　A method of computing depreciation by determining loss in rental value attributable to a depreciated item and applying a gross rent multiplier to that figure.

cash equivalency technique　Method of adjusting a sales price downward to reflect the increase in value caused by the assumption or procurement by the buyer of a loan at an interest rate lower than the prevailing market rate.

change, principle of　The principle that no physical or economic condition ever remains constant.

chattel　Personal property items, which thus are not considered part of the real estate on which they are located.

client　One who hires another person as a representative or an agent for a fee.

compaction　Matted down or compressed extra soil that may be added to a lot to fill in the low areas or raise the level of the parcel.

comparables　Properties that are substantially equivalent to the subject property in their design, size, location and quality of construction.

competition, principle of　The principle that a successful business attracts other such businesses, which will dilute profits.

condemnation　Taking private property for public use through court action under the government's right of eminent domain, with just compensation to the owner.

conditions, covenants and restrictions (CC&Rs)　Private limitations on property use placed in the deed received by the property owner, typically by reference to a Declaration of Restrictions recorded for an entire subdivision.

condominium　The absolute ownership of space, referred to as a *unit,* generally in a multiunit building, by a legal description of the airspace that the unit actually occupies, plus an undivided interest in the ownership of the *common elements,* which are owned jointly with the other condominium unit owners. The condominium form of ownership is used both for residential and commercial properties.

conformity, principle of The principle that buildings should be similar in design, construction and age to other buildings in the neighborhood to reach their highest value.

contiguous Adjacent parcels of land.

contract rent Rent being paid by agreement between lessor (landlord) and lessee (tenant).

contribution, principle of The principle that any improvement to property, whether to vacant land or to a building, is worth only what it adds to the property's market value, regardless of the improvement's construction cost.

cooperative A multiunit residential building with title in a trust or corporation that is owned by and operated for the benefit of persons living within it, who are the beneficial owners of the trust or the stockholders of the corporation, each possessing a proprietary lease.

cost approach The process of estimating the value of real estate by adding the appraiser's estimate of the reproduction or replacement cost of the property improvements, less the amount by which they have depreciated, to the estimated land value.

cost index Number representing the construction cost at a particular time in relation to the cost at an earlier time, prepared by a cost-reporting or indexing service.

CPE Certified Personalty Evaluator, International Association of Assessing Officers.

CRA Certified Review Appraiser, National Association of Review Appraisers and Mortgage Underwriters.

CREA Certified Real Estate Appraiser, National Association of Real Estate Appraisers.

cubic-foot method Method of estimating building reproduction cost by multiplying the number of cubic feet of space the building encloses by the current construction cost per cubic foot.

curable depreciation A depreciated item that can be restored or replaced economically.

data Information pertinent to a specific appraisal assignment. Data may be *general* (relating to the economy, region, city and neighborhood) or *specific* (relating to the subject property and comparable properties in the market area).

decreasing returns, law of The principle that states that property reaches a point at which additional improvements no longer bring a corresponding increase in property income or value.

deed A written instrument that conveys title to or an interest in real estate when executed and delivered properly.

deed restrictions Clauses in a deed to real estate limiting the future uses of the property. Deed restrictions may limit the number of buildings, their design and the quality of their construction. Deed restrictions may affect the property rights appraised favorably or unfavorably, depending on existing uses of the subject and nearby properties.

depreciated cost The reproduction or replacement cost of a building, less accrued depreciation to the time of the appraisal.

depreciation Loss in value from any cause, including physical deterioration, functional obsolescence and external obsolescence.

depth factor An adjustment factor applied to the value per front foot of lots that vary from the standard depth.

direct costs Construction costs that are involved with either site preparation or building construction, including fixtures.

disposal field A drainage area, which should not be close to the water supply, where waste from a septic tank is dispersed into the ground through tile and gravel.

easement A right to use the land of someone else for a specific purpose, which as a right-of-way or for utility lines. An easement is a *nonpossessory* interest in land; this means that the holder of an easement owns a right of use only and not any portion of the underlying land. An *easement appurtenant* passes with the land when the land is conveyed.

economic life The period of time during which a structure may reasonably be expected to perform the function for which it was designed or intended.

economic obsolescence (*See* external obsolescence.)

effective age The age of a building based on the actual wear and tear and maintenance, or lack of it, that the building has received.

effective gross income Income from all sources, less anticipated vacancy and collection losses.

egress The right to leave a tract of land to reach a public way.

eminent domain The right of a government or quasi-public body to acquire private property for public use through a court action called *condemnation*. The court determines whether the use is a public one and what the compensation paid to the owner should be.

encroachment A building, wall or fence that extends beyond the land of the owner and illegally intrudes on the land of an adjoining owner or a public street or alley.

encumbrance Any lien (such as a mortgage, tax lien or judgment lien),

easement, restriction on the use of land, outstanding dower right or other interest that may diminish the market value of real estate.

environmental obsolescence (*See* external obsolescence.)

equalization The raising or lowering of assessed values for real property tax purposes in a particular county or taxing district to make them equal to assessments in other counties or districts.

equity The interest or value that an owner has in real estate over and above any mortgage against it.

escalator clause A clause in a contract, lease or mortgage providing for increases in wages, rent or interest, based on fluctuations in certain economic indexes, costs or taxes.

escheat The process by which the property of a decedent dying *intestate* (without a will) and without heirs reverts to the state.

estate The degree, quantity, nature and extent of interest that a person has in real estate.

excess income (*See* excess rent.)

excess rent The difference between the market rent and the contract rent, when the market rent is lower.

expense Outlay of money chargeable against income.

externalities, principle of The principle that holds that factors outside a property can influence property value. Outside factors that can affect property values range from upkeep of neighboring properties to economic and political factors such as interest rates.

external obsolescence Loss in value from forces outside the building or property, such as changes in optimum land use, legislative enactments that restrict or impair property rights and changes in supply-demand relationships. Also called *environmental* or *economic obsolescence*.

Federal Reserve Bank System   Central bank of the United States established to regulate the flow of money and the cost of credit (borrowing).

fee simple   The greatest possible estate or right of ownership of real property, continuing without time limitation. Sometimes called *fee* or *fee simple absolute*.

FHA   Federal Housing Administration, which insures loans made by approved lenders in accordance with its regulations.

final value estimate   The appraiser's estimate of the defined value of the subject property, arrived at by reconciling the estimates of value derived from the cost, income capitalization and sales comparison approaches.

fixed expenses   Those costs that are more or less permanent and do not vary in relation to the property's income, such as real estate taxes and insurance for fire, theft and hazards.

fixture   Anything attached to the land and considered part of the real estate, including things that once were personal property but are attached to real estate in such a way that they cannot be easily removed. An exception is made for *trade fixtures*, which are installed for commercial purposes under the terms of a lease and can be removed on termination of the lease.

foreclosure   A court action initiated by the mortgagee (lender), or a lienor, to have the court order that the debtor's real estate be sold to pay the mortgage or other lien, such as a mechanic's lien or judgment.

front foot   A standard of measurement, which is a strip of land one foot wide fronting on the street and extending the depth of the lot. Value may be quoted per front foot.

frost line   The depth of frost penetration in the soil. The frost line varies through the United States, and foundation footings should be placed below this depth to prevent movement of the structure.

functional obsolescence   Defects in a building or structure that detract from its value or marketability, usually the result of layout, design or other features that are less desirable than features designed for the same functions in newer property. Functional obsolescence is described as *curable* when the physical or design features that no longer are considered desirable by property buyers can be replaced or redesigned at low cost. Functional obsolescence is described as *incurable* if the currently undesirable features are not easily remedied or economically justified.

gradient   The slope, or rate of change in elevation, of a surface, road or pipe. Gradient is expressed in inches of rise or fall per horizontal linear foot of ascent or descent.

gross income   A property's total potential income from all sources during a specified period of time.

gross income multiplier   A figure used as a multiplier of the gross income of a property from all sources to produce an estimate of the property's value. Usually used with commercial real estate.

gross rent multiplier   A figure used as a multiplier of the gross rental income of a property to produce an estimate of the property's value. Usually used with single-family residences.

ground lease   A lease for *land only* on which the tenant usually owns or is to construct a building, as specified by the lease. Such leases are usually long-term net leases; that is, the tenant pays all or most of the expenses associated with ownership of the real estate, such as property taxes.

GSA Graduate Senior Appraiser, National Residential Appraisers Institute.

highest and best use Historically, that legally and physically possible use of land that produces the highest land (or property) value. A *highest and best use study* considers the balance of site and improvements as well as the intensity and length of nearby uses.

historical cost Actual cost of a building at the time it was constructed.

historical rent Contract rent paid in past years.

HUD Department of Housing and Urban Development.

IAAO International Association of Assessing Officers.

IFA Member, National Association of Independent Fee Appraisers, Inc.

improvements on land Alterations or structures of whatever nature, usually privately rather than publicly owned, erected on a site to enable its utilization; for example, buildings, fences, driveways and retaining walls.

improvement to land Usually a public work, or one publicly dedicated, such as a curb, sidewalk, street-lighting system or sewer, constructed to enable the development of privately owned land.

income capitalization approach The process of estimating the value of an income-producing property by capitalization of the annual net operating income expected to be produced by the property during its remaining useful life.

increasing returns, law of The principle that additional property improvements increase property income or value.

incurable depreciation A depreciated item that would be impossible or too expensive to restore or replace.

indirect costs Construction costs that do not involve either site preparation or building erection; for example, building permit, land survey, overhead expenses such as insurance and payroll taxes, and builder's profit.

industrial district or park A controlled parklike development designed to accommodate specific types of industry, providing public utilities, streets, railroad sidings, water and sewage facilities.

ingress The right to enter a tract of land. Often used interchangeably with the term *access*.

installment contract A contract for the sale of real estate by which the purchase price is paid in installments over an extended period of time by the purchaser, who is in possession, with the title retained by the seller until a certain number of payments are made.

interest The cost of credit. A percentage of the principal amount of a loan charged by a lender for its use, usually expressed as an annual rate.

interest rate Return of an investment, consisting of four component rates: *safe rate* (interest rate paid on investments of maximum security, highest liquidity and minimum risk); *risk rate* (addition to safe rate to compensate for the hazards that accompany investments in real estate); *nonliquidity rate* (penalty charged for the time needed to convert real estate into cash); and *management rate* (compensation to the owner for the work involved in managing an investment and reinvesting the funds received from the property).

land The earth's surface in its natural condition, extending down to the center of the globe, its surface and all things affixed to it, and the airspace above the surface to navigable airspace.

land capitalization rate The rate of return, including interest on the land only.

landlocked parcel   A parcel of land without access to any type of public road.

landlord   One who owns property and leases it to a tenant. Also called the *lessor*.

land residual technique   A method of capitalization using the net income remaining to the land after return on and recapture of the building value have been deducted.

latent defect   Physical deficiency or construction defect not readily ascertainable from a reasonable inspection of the property, such as a defective septic tank or underground sewage system, or improper plumbing or electrical wiring.

lease   A written or oral contract for the possession of a landlord's (lessor's) property for a stipulated period of time in consideration for the payment of rent by the tenant (lessee). Leases for more than one year generally must be in writing.

legal description   A statement identifying land by a system prescribed by law.

levy   To impose or assess a tax on a person or property; the amount of taxes to be imposed in a given district.

loft   An atticlike space below the roof of a house or barn; any of the upper stories of a warehouse or factory.

lot and block system   A method of legal description of an individual parcel of land by reference to tract, block and lot numbers and other information by which the parcel is identified in a recorded subdivision map. Also called *lot, block and tract system* and *subdivision system*.

MAI   Member designation of the Appraisal Institute.

maintenance expenses   Costs incurred for day-to-day upkeep, such as management wages and benefits of building employees, fuel, utility services, decorating and repairs.

market price   (*See* sales price.)

market rent   An estimate of a property's rent potential, that is, what an investor can expect to receive in rental income.

market value   The most probable price real estate should bring in a sale occurring under normal market conditions.

mechanic's lien   A lien created by statute that exists in favor of contractors, laborers or materialmen who have performed work or furnished materials in the erection or repair of a building. Also includes architects, engineers, landscapers and truckers.

metes and bounds description   A method of legal description specifying the perimeter of a parcel of land by use of measured distances from a point of beginning along specified boundaries, or bounds, using monuments, or markers, as points of reference.

MFLA   Master Farm and Land Appraiser, National Association of Master Appraisers.

mile   A measurement of distance: 1,760 yards or 5,280 feet.

mobile home   A structure transportable in one or more sections, designed and equipped to contain not more than two dwelling units to be used with or without a foundation system; does not include a recreational vehicle. Also called a *manufactured home*.

NAIFA   National Association of Independent Fee Appraisers, Inc.

NAR   National Association of REALTORS®.

NARAMU   National Association of Review Appraisers and Mortgage Underwriters.

NAREA   National Association of Real Estate Appraisers.

neighborhood   A residential or commercial area with similar types of properties, buildings of similar value or age, predominant land-use activities and natural or fabricated geographic boundaries, such as highways or rivers.

neighborhood life cycle The period during which most of the properties in a neighborhood undergo the following three stages: *development* (growth), in which improvements are made and properties experience rising demand and value, *equilibrium*, in which properties undergo little change; and *decline*, in which properties become less desirable and require an increasing amount of upkeep to retain their original utility.

net lease A lease requiring the tenant to pay rent and all the costs of maintaining the building, including property taxes, insurance, repairs and other expenses of ownership. Sometimes known as an *absolute net lease* or *triple net lease*.

net operating income Income remaining after operating expenses are deducted from effective gross income.

nonconforming use A property use that is permitted to continue after a zoning ordinance prohibiting it has been established for the area; a use that differs sharply from the prevailing uses in a neighborhood.

observed-condition depreciation A method of computing depreciation in which the appraiser estimates the loss in value for all items of depreciation.

obsolescence Lessening of value from out-of-date features (property design, construction materials or use) that no longer are desired by property buyers. Obsolescence is an element of depreciation.

occupancy rate The percentage of total rental units occupied and producing income.

operating expenses The cost of all goods and services used or consumed in the process of obtaining and maintaining income. (*See* maintenance expenses, fixed expenses and reserves for replacement.)

operating statement The written record of a business's gross income, expenses and resulting net income.

option A right given for a valuable consideration to purchase or lease property at a future date for a specified price and terms. The right may or may not be exercised at the option holder's discretion.

orientation Positioning a structure on its lot considering its exposure to the sun and prevailing winds, and the need for privacy and protection from noise.

overall rate The direct ratio between a property's annual net income and its sales price.

overimprovement An improvement to property that is not likely to contribute its cost to the total market value of the property.

percentage lease A lease commonly used for commercial property that provides for a rental based on the tenant's gross sales on the premises. It generally stipulates a base monthly rental, plus a percentage of any gross sales exceeding a certain amount.

personal property Movable objects called *chattel* that are not permanently attached to real estate and thus are not transferred when the real estate is sold.

physical deterioration—curable Loss of value caused by neglected repair or maintenance that is economically feasible and would result in an increase in market value equal to or exceeding the cost to cure.

physical deterioration—incurable Loss of value caused by neglected repairs or maintenance of building components that would not contribute comparable value to a building if corrected.

physical life   The length of time a structure can physically exist without regard to its economic use.

planned unit development (PUD)   A subdivision consisting of individually owned residential and/or commercial parcels or lots as well as areas owned in common.

plottage value   The subsequent increase in the unit values of a group of adjacent properties when they are combined into one property. Also called *assemblage*.

point of beginning   The place at which a legal description of land using the metes and bounds method starts.

prepaid items of expense   Expense items, such as insurance premiums and tax reserves, that have been paid in advance of the time that the expense is incurred. Prepaid expenses are prorated and credited to the seller when preparing a closing statement.

price   The amount of money set or paid as the consideration in the sale of an item at a particular time.

profit and loss statement   (*See* operating statement.)

progression, principle of   The principle that states that the value of a property will be greater when it is surrounded by properties that are in better condition than it would be if it is surrounded by properties in equally good or worse condition.

property residual technique   A method of capitalization using the net operating income remaining to the property as a whole.

quantity survey method   A method for finding the reproduction cost of a building in which the costs of erecting or installing all of the component parts of a new building, including both direct and indirect costs, are added.

real estate   Land; a portion of the earth's surface extending downward to the center of the earth and upward into space, including fixtures permanently attached thereto by nature or by man, anything incidental or appurtenant to land and anything immovable by law.

real property   The rights of ownership associated with real estate; also used interchangeably with the term *real estate*.

recapture rate   The percentage of a property's original cost that is returned to the owner as income during the remaining economic life of the investment.

reconciliation   The final step in the appraisal process, in which the appraiser reconciles the estimates of value received from the cost, income capitalization and sales comparison approaches to value, to arrive at a final estimate of market value for the subject property.

reconstruction of the operating statement   The process of eliminating the inapplicable types of expense items for appraisal purposes and adjusting the remaining valid expenses if necessary.

rectangular survey system   A method of legal description of real estate established in 1785 by the federal government, by which land is referenced by proximity to *principal meridians* and *base lines*. Also called the *U.S. government survey system* and the *section and township system*.

regional multipliers   Adjustment factors by which standard cost figures can be multiplied to allow for regional price differences.

regression, principle of   The principle that states that the value of property will not be as great when it is surrounded by properties that are in poorer condition, as it would be if it is surrounded by properties in equally good or better condition.

remaining economic life   The number of years of useful life left to a building from the date of appraisal, that is, the remaining number of years in which it can be used for its intended purpose.

rent-loss method of depreciation   (*See* capitalized value method.)

replacement cost   The current construction cost of a building with exactly the same utility as the subject property.

reproduction cost   The current construction cost of an exact duplicate of the subject building, using the same materials and techniques.

reserves for replacement   Allowances set up for replacement of building and equipment items that have a relatively short life expectancy.

residual   In appraising, the value remaining after all deductions have been made.

right-of-way   The right that one has to pass across the land of another; an *easement*.

risk rate   (*See* interest rate.)

rod   A measure of length, 16½ feet.

RRA   Registered Review Appraiser (Canada), National Association of Review Appraisers and Mortgage Underwriters.

safe rate   (*See* interest rate.)

sales comparison approach   The process of estimating the market value of property through the examination and comparison of actual sales of comparable properties. Also called the *market data approach*.

sales price   The actual selling price of a property.

site   Land suitable for building purposes, usually by the addition of utilities or other services.

special assessment   A charge against real estate made by a unit of government to cover the proportionate cost of an improvement, such as a street or sewer.

special purpose property   Property that has unique usage requirements, such as a church or a museum, making it difficult to convert to another use.

square foot method   A method for finding the reproduction cost of a building in which the cost per square foot of a recently built comparable structure is multiplied by the number of square feet in the subject property.

SRA   Residential appraiser designation, Appraisal Institute.

SR/WA   Member designation, International Right of Way Association.

straight-line method of depreciation   A method of computing depreciation in which the cost of a building is depreciated at a fixed annual percentage rate; also called the *age-life method*.

straight-line recapture   A method of capital recapture in which total accrued depreciation is spread over the useful life of a building in equal amounts.

subdivision   A tract of land divided by the owner into blocks, building lots and streets by a recorded subdivision plat. Compliance with local regulations is required.

substitution, principle of   The basic appraisal premise that the market value of real estate is influenced by the cost of acquiring a substitute or comparable property.

summation method   Another term for the cost approach to appraising.

supply and demand, principle of   The principle that the value of a commodity will rise as demand increases and/or supply decreases.

survey   The process of measuring land to determine its size, location and physical description; also, the map or plat showing the results of a survey.

tenant   One who has possession of real estate. In the broad sense, an owner of any kind of right or title (tenant in common); in the limited sense, a lessee (month-to-month tenant). The estate or interest held is called a *tenancy*.

time-share   An estate (ownership) or use interest in real property for only a designated time period each year. Usually measured in weekly increments. Because of high initial marketing costs, time-share units in some areas have shown little or no appreciation at the time of resale.

title   The evidence of a person's right to the ownership and possession of land.

topography   Surface features of land; elevation, ridges, slope, contour.

trade fixtures   Articles of personal property installed by a tenant under the terms of a lease. Trade fixtures are removable by the tenant before the lease expires.

underimprovement   An improvement to real estate that is less than the property's highest and best use; for example, a single-family house built on a lot zoned for a six-unit residential building.

unit-in-place method   A method for finding the reproduction cost of a building in which the construction cost per square foot of each component part of the subject building (including material, labor, overhead and builder's profit) is multiplied by the number of

square feet of the component part in the subject building.

useful life   The period of time during which a structure may reasonably be expected to perform the function for which it was designed or intended.

use value   The value of a property designed to fit the specific requirements of the owner but which would have little or no use to another owner. Also referred to as *value-in-use*.

vacancy and collection losses   (*See* allowance for vacancy and collection losses.)

valuation principles   Factors that affect market value, such as the principles of substitution, highest and best use, supply and demand, conformity, progression, regression, contribution, increasing and decreasing returns, competition, change, stage of life cycle and anticipation.

value   The power to command other goods in exchange; the present worth of future rights to income and benefits arising from ownership.

vendee   Buyer.

vendor   Seller.

way   A street, alley or other thoroughfare or easement permanently established for passage of persons or vehicles.

yield   Income on an investment. Usually used to refer to equity investments.

zoning ordinance   Regulation of the character and use of property by a municipality or county through the exercise of its police power.

Index